# WALKING IN THE LIGHT...

*Poetry and Essays*
*Reflecting Life Experiences*
*As Seen Through the Eyes*
*of a Cancer Survivor*

*By*

*Blaine Thorson*

Published by Speranza, LLC
P.O. Box 2282
Kalamazoo, MI  49003

ISBN  0-9674740-5-1

Printed by Central Plains Book Manufacturing
U.S.A.

# TABLE OF CONTENTS

# PART ONE

# PART TWO

Blaine Thorson was born July 14th, 1935. In May, 1953, he graduated from Logan High school in La Crosse, Wisconsin. He personally reflected on his educational background... "Unknown and undetected, I was born color blind. I was subsequently tagged as a slow learner, if not somewhat retarded, by my Kindergarten, First and Second Grade teachers. I believed their assessment as well, and did not burn up any scholastic paths. In fact, I didn't know I wasn't educationally handicapped until I attended my first Navy school, which consisted of a fourteen month course compressed into six months."

Work History: Worked at various jobs (farming, mechanic, honey wagon, carpenter) through high school. Between high school and joining the Navy Blaine worked in construction for one year with building, brick laying, roofing, plumbing, and electrics. He also worked for Trane Company for three months as a welder.

US Navy: July, 1954 through August, 1958

10 week Recruit training at Great Lakes, IL: automatic promotion to Seaman Apprentice (E-2) six month Telecommunication school at Bainbridge, MD: Learned typing, international Morse Code (30 WPM), theory of operation and networking of all major communication equipment used by the Navy on ships, land, sea, undersea, landing craft or aircraft.

Served onboard one ship for 3 years and 4 months. Nominated by two Commanding Officers for a fleet appointment to the US Naval Academy and then was disqualified due to color blindness. Color blindness also later prevented Blaine from achieving a battle field commission and participating in any enlisted positions. This kept him from warrant and other officer programs.

Promoted to the Rank of RM1 (E-6) in three and a half years through fleet wide testing (written) of all eligible applicants for open billets E-3 through E-6. A 600 pound work bench broke loose during a North Atlantic gale, delivering a Karate chop to Blaines lower back and pinning him against a radio receiver bank he was working on.

Between enlistments- August- October, 1958: Due to hostilities in Lebanon, Blaine's enlistment was extended 90 days for the convenience of the government. His entrance for fall enrollment to college was canceled and resubmitted for spring. However, he was released and discharged only two weeks past his original enlistment. He returned to the construction field as a heavy equipment operator and reapplied to college. Unfortunately, he lost his priority to class scheduling and every day saw a change to his class schedule or selections. In addition, his back injury prevented his return to the building trade.

US Navy: October, 1958 through October, 1979

Attended teletype repair school, advanced electronic repair school, Instructor training. Served onboard twelve ships (8 when assigned to 2 Admiral staffs) with 26 months spent in VietNam waters. Also involved with 2 major communication stations and two Navy schools. Served as Department Director and Command Master Chief at one of the communications stations and one of the schools.

Promoted to Chief (E-7) with seven and one half years total service, Senior Chief (E-8) in 11 years, and Master Chief (E-9) after 16 years. The Navy average is 13 years for E-7, 18 years for E-8, and 26 years for E-9.

On retirement from the Navy, Blaine applied for a teaching position with the San Diego Community College District (SDCCD) in their Telecommunication technical training program. He was offered and accepted an Associate Dean position managing from 14-21 teachers with degrees up to and including the Doctorate level. He held that position for eight years until Proposition 13 cut back and eliminated his job.

During the last two years at SDCCD, Blaine established a business to install Satellite Receive Only TV systems in homes and businesses. He also provided data linking via satellite and wire consultation services to larger corporations. A move back to Wisconsin to be centrally located did not prove to be fruitful. Shortly after the relocation, it was discovered that exposure to agent orange while in VietNam waters, 19 years of working in soundproof, windowless high security areas, and breathing asbestos dust knocked out of the overhead when guns were fired or missiles launched had caught up with him.

When the nodule on Blaine's left lung proved to be cancer, a VA oncology doctor explained his options, underlining it with the statistics that only 1 per cent survive. She asked what he wanted to do. Blaine said that the first thing he would do was pray for the other 99 per cent. Radiation was recommended. In lieu of driving back and forth to Madison, WI four nights of every week for three months, he elected to seek radiation treatment locally.

Doctors recommended surgery to remove the affected part of Blaine's lung. Unfortunately, things did not go well. The 5th and 6th ribs were removed, and the lower part of his rib cage caved in. Now, instead of protecting the intestines, the ribs irritate them when Blaine sits upright. He has experienced the busted rib pain every day of his life since then. In addition, his left vocal cords were cut, the tendons and nerve endings controlling his shoulder blade and supporting his ribs were severed, and the entire left lung was removed. In an effort to destroy any stray cells by radiation treatment, "over radiation" occurred, which softened his bones and lead to osteoporosis. After 10 years of being cancer free, the right lung developed an active nodule. Taking a biopsy may collapse the lung, and removing the infected area would put Blaine on an oxygen machine for the rest of his life. He was told that Chemotherapy was not normally effective on slow growing cancers like his, and he is doubtful of whether or not his body could handle any more radiation. With restricted options, all he can do is wait and see how fast it will grow.

To the true poet or ciritc, at first glance, some of these poems will appear poorly written or structured, and rightly so. However, might I suggest, like singing the national anthem or reciting the Pledge of Allegiance, repetition will capture the feeling and enhance the message which the words are intended to convey without any presupposed glitter or glamour.

It has been a pleasant and comforting pastime for me to reflect on some of what God has given us. The most important of which was His only begotten Son, Jesus, for the redemption of our sins, and the Bible as a guide post for our walk in the light. He is here for us, from our entrance into this corrupt world, prepared for the fight, with our little hands clinched tight into a fist, to our departure from this terrestrial shell with the palm outstretched toward heaven in humble resignation.

How we spend our DASH (the time between birth and mortal death) and the footprints we leave behind in the sands of time is a choice given to us by God. In all of creation, mankind is the only species given the option between right and wrong... Eternal Glory, or Eternal Ruin; Heaven or Hell; one or the other. How can you not be excited being a Christian (a follower of Christ), an exalted priviledge given to mankind? To accept and follow the way of life Christ taught means peace of mind, contentment, forgiveness, happiness, hope, life abundant here and now, and life that shall never end. What else is there? What more could there be? It is obvious even to the most casual observer that mankind will experience mortal death. Oh, how I wish all would embrace Christinaity!

What a grand and glorious day it would be if we could all march to the same drummer (that which is taught in the Bible) without any additions or subtrac- tions, able to walk into any church meeting place and hear the same unaltered message from God. Please investigate the Scripture references included with some of the poems. It is with profound but humble gratitude and adoration that I thank God for this opportunity to share these poems. I trust they put some of His prolific words in perspective, and that they will help to demonstrate that the Bible is not difficult to understand. I hope they will encourage your spiritual growth and awareness of God working in your life. Most importantly, I pray these poems will provide you with encouragement in times of sickness or despair, comfort in times of duress, and solace and peace of mind in your loss.

Blaine Thorson

In certain intellectual circles there is a widely held view that the Bible is just a story of man's search for God. These people believe that the Bible is not inspired, but rather what man imagines about God. In this way the Bible is reduced to the level of an ordinary book pretending to be Divine. Throughout history, men have referred to stories in the Bible, and have shown the importance of the Bible in terms of people's lives, cultures, and nations.

Is it our destiny to dwell in a world that is tragically and pathetically divided religiously forever? Jesus' followers are divided into various sects in excess of 300 conflicting and contradicting doctrines. There are many reasons offered for this division, with the Bible taking the blunt of the negative conversations. Some try to convince you that "the Bible Mystery is difficult to understand." "You will get confused if you try to read it." However, the Bible emphatically and plainly teaches that we can now fully understand God's plan for mankind. The "mystery" of the Kingdom of Heaven has been revealed through the disciples (see Matthew 13:11). As prophesied in the Old Testament, the disciples would be "trees of righteousness, the planting of the Lord, that He might be glorified" (see Isaiah 61:3). Christ, telling the disciples about the coming of the Comforter, summarized by saying, "Herein is my Father glorified, that you bear much fruit, so shall you be my disciples" (see John 15:8). There is an abundance of fruit in the New Testament for you to savor and enjoy for the Mystery is explained (see Ephesians 3: 4-11). "All Scripture is given by inspiration of God and is profitable for doctrine, for reproof, for correction (self discipline), for instruction unto righteousness (see 11 Timothy 3:16). God sent His Son to show us a better way: these were the first "How To" books (see Hebrews 1:1,2). It is important that we know the truth, for it will set us free (see John 8:31,32).

Will our Christian leaders ever have the courage to fess up, abort the superfluous pageantry, and return to the simple teachings of Christ? Are they so entrenched that they fit in the category of the blind leading the blind (see Matthew 15:14)? How can they read Scripture, or be told they are wrong, and still return to teaching error to face the consequences (see II Peter 2:21,22)? Knowing full well from time Beginning to time End they are not in God's favor making changes to His doctrine (see Deuteronomy 12:32 and Revelation 22:18). It does not take a rocket scientist to realize Adam and Eve committed the first sin by not doing what God told them to do! We can only imagine their fate if they kept returning to eat the forbidden fruit.

There is, of course, a marked difference between the Bible and regular books. While I am certain there are many books, including this one, that God has helped to write, not even the most zealous modern author would claim that God told them what to write. For the Bible, on the other hand, we can make and support that claim. The contents were put in place over thousands of years, yet maintain continuity. While the 66 books were written by many different humans, the golden threads that run through the Bible, from beginning to end, certainly document that God dictated the inspired words, directed and supervised the writing. The 39 books of the Old Testament harmonize with each other and many intertwine with the 27 books of the New Testament, which also support and harmonize with each other. This is akin to building a super highway coast to coast. While many construction firms will be involved, there can be only one architect- one major and controlling plan, lest there be thousands of miles of road leading to nowhere. Where else can you find a 66 book library you can carry in your hands? Where else can you find one book in which you can read about all things pertaining to life and obtain answers to the most complex issues confronting you? (see II Peter 1:3)

Simply put, the Old Testament is an account of a Nation, nurtured by God, which was selected to prepare the world for the coming of a Man. The New Testament is an account of that Man, Jesus the Christ.

# WALKING
# IN THE
# LIGHT...

# REFLECTIONS
## ON
## LIFE...

# DAILY THANKS

The warm soft touch of a summer breeze,
as it dances through the trees.
The song of a blue bird, from our window sill,
or the evening call of the Whipper Will.

In harmony the crickets chirp and frogs sing,
announcing good things the day will bring.
From morn to dusk what could be sweeter,
than watching birds at the feeder?

Listening to the field and sweet corn grow,
waiting to harvest what we sow.
Nature providing ample sun and rain blends,
filling in bare spots until it ends.

For all the choices of food we have to eat,
all the good folks we get to meet.
Our prosperity, jobs and household chore,
this day of grace and so many more.

Destiny's road or path in our life's highway,
sets our course each day and every night.
No matter who or what we think is our lot,
Give it your best with this only chance we' ve got!

## THE QUESTION

How can something end that has not begun,
or lose when no one has won?
What can progress have a chance to bring,
if we don't contribute anything?

Life takes a lot of personal caring,
constant giving and sharing.
Giving more love back than we are receiving,
open and honest with no deceiving.

Accepting this life cause it just has to be,
a growing ground for you and me.
It will not be easy and in that we can trust,
looking ahead a necessary must.

Learn from history that we can gain,
a lesson or two we may sustain.
Learning to make today and every tomorrow,
better for us and from those we borrow.

# WHO AM I?

When I look into a mirror, who do I really see?
Is that image reflecting back an individual who is me?
Is it who I think it is, or who people say?
Can I be honest with that question or address it another day?

How can we tread through life totally unaware,
what people are telling us with that naked glare.
We continue on the way we are and never change a bit,
displaying our narrow mindedness, no matter where it might hit.

Trying to convince the world in our every wail,
not knowing it is body language that tips the scale.
Childish self-centered attitudes we cannot let go,
emitting meaningless words from mouths that actions do not show.

We speak of love for one another with concern and care,
turn around and do our own thing as though they were not there.
Hurrying and scurrying to manipulate self-serving result,
lying and justifying so it ends up someone else's fault.

Even the little things encompass our self-seeking dimension,
it isn't the words but the outcome that projects our intention.
The thing that will bother me till the very end,
destroying another chance for happiness, and still we do not bend!

(See James 1:23, 24 and 3:16
and I Corinthians 13:12)

6

## OUR HANDS

We are born with hands clenched tight,
as though prepared for the internal fight.
Unsuspecting at this start in life,
of the fight from within or other strife.

At birth, God's spirit is given to us alone,
His plan in a Bible we'll be shown.
The struggle of self, loose or win,
His spirit will return to him again.

We have the choice on how to travel,
worldly devices or God's work unravel.
Put our intelligence to good use,
achieving salvation's plan or eternal abuse.

As mortal death closes our eyes,
our palms will open toward the skies.
We will know our earthly days are done,
the race over and if we have won.

(See Genesis 2:7, Luke 16:22-25,
Ecclesiates 3:21, Romans 6:16 and 7:14-25,
and I Corinthians 13:12)

## TREES OF RIGHTEOUSNESS

The next time you look at a furniture ad,
note the wood that makes them so glad,
They proudly proclaim it's a Northern wood,
formed and polished only as a craftsman could.
But why is this, we should boldly ask,
isn't all wood given the same task?

Look at the trees of a Southern forest so green,
plenty of sunshine, rain and no season that's lean.
Growing without struggle from God's fertile ground,
taking on shape but no character can be found.
Its loose graining and abundant pulpy mass,
will not stand scrutiny of a workmen's glass.

Let's take a lesson from that great Northern Pine,
with snow laden branches in winter recline.
The contrasting heat of summers' hot glare,
from swamping rain to a dry arid air.
Soil washed away to expose life support roots,
removing nutrients from newly formed roots.

In spite of hostile elements of nature's hardship,
it grows straight and true with nary a slip.
Its life rings gathered in close-knit bound,
consistent in beauty in their go around.
The graining sturdy in their varied cluster,
to provide strength and workmen's luster.
That struggle produced a highly prized wood,
just as our life in Christ surely should.

Of course the Burl Oak is the most prized treasure,
a knurled surface reflecting its life measure.
Beneath the distorted and twisted knots of plenty,
lies a strong and beautiful grain not found in many.
The tribulation and struggle for life from it grew,
a treasure from God just like me and like you.

8

# Trees of Righteousness Explained

The title of this poem comes from Isaiah 61:3, "that they may be called trees of righteousness, the planting of the Lord, that He may be glorified." A prophesy that is confirmed in John 15:8 as Christ, talking to the apostles about the coming of the Comforter, summerizes by saying, "Herein is my Father glorified, that you bear much fruit; so shall you be my disciples." This poem is a summary of the many fruits that are given to us in the New Testament to increase our understanding of the pain and suffering we experience in our lifetime.

Does God cause suffering? Does God punish some and not others? Psalm 97:2 tells us, "clouds and darkness surround him, righteousness and justice are the foundation of His throne!" James 1:13 tells us God doesn't tempt anyone. James 1:17 tells us that every good gift comes from above. Matthew 5:45 explains that our Father which is in Heaven, "maketh His son rise on the evil and on the good, and sendeth rain on the just and the unjust."

We can identify the source of suffering by reviewing a few Scriptures. John 13:2 explains that the devil put into the heart of Judas to betray Christ. Paul tells us in II Corinthians 12:7 that his "thorn in the flesh" was the messanger of Satan to buffet him, lest he should be exalted above measure. In verse 8, Paul states that he besought the Lord three times that it would depart from him. The response came in verse nine, when we read, "My grace is sufficient for thee; for my strength is made perfect in weakness."

Pain is necessary lest we continue to hurt ourselves- sickness is necessary to stimulate research. More important, the Hebrew writer tells us in Hebrews 2:10 that, "for it become him, for whom are all things, and by whom are all things, in bringing many sons unto glory, to make the captain of their salvation perfect through suffering." Also we read about putting others before ourselves (in Philipians 2:3,4), carrying others' burdens (in Galatians 6:2) and discovering that it is better to give than receive (in Acts 20:35). We can also acquire a greater appreciation of fellowship (in Phillipians ..... and gain a new appreciation for redemption (in Romans 8: 28-39).

Paul tells us, "for our light affliction, which is but for a moment, worketh for us a far more exceeding and eternal weight of glory" (in II Corinthians 4:17). Our life is but a speck when we compare it to the eternity that follows. We are best served by forgetting those things that are behind, and reach forth on to those things which are before (Philipians 3:13). Instead, we can hone our positive thinking by concentrating on, "whatsoever things are true, whatsoever things are honest, whatsoever things are just, pure, lovely, are of good report; if there be any virtue, and if there be any praise, think on these things" (Philipians 4:8). And more important, in whatever state we are, be content (see Philippians 4: 11). After all, if this life was perfect, what would there be to look forward to? Would Heaven have the same appeal?

## TODAY

My, oh my, just what can I do,
to remove this feeling blue?
Try and try even though I may,
to succeed each and every day;
It seems happiness and success,
always end up being a mess.

I need to stop for a short while,
and look at life with a smile.
Reorganize a few ways of doing,
to minimize my future stewing.
Increase my lifes' daily treasure
equal to my personal measure.

Fashion thoughts for a positive day,
keep negative out in every way.
Appreciate all facets of this life,
set aside the self-made strife.
Realize that all things that befall,
are controlled by me after all!

Everything will come out all right,
if I employ self powers' might.
I can't place blame onto others,
envy friend, sister or brother.
No matter what the total outcome,
it's my product and my sum.

Live this day as though my last,
and put yesterday in the past.
View tomorrow though it may not come,
for it's not promised to anyone.
If I indeed do this day right,
I'll be ready through the night.

Whatever I want my life to be,
it must start first with me.
If I want success to come and stay,
I must start now without delay.
Give this life its very best shot
with this only chance I've got.

(See Phillipians 3:13 and 4:11-13)

# THE TONGUE

A person's tongue is a mighty force,
changing history and its course.
The wagging tongue is Satan's work,
in the busybody he always lurks.
The Bible teaches to what's inside,
and not how the other should abide.

Words spoken to another about someone,
what they did or haven't done;
Not something for a Christians' ears,
and from Heaven they will bring no cheers.

When you point a finger at one who lacks,
please observe the three pointing back,
and the thumb pointing back;
and God, who will one day ask why.

The Bible will put them on track,
and they will see what they lack.
It doesn't help for us to criticize,
and our own salvation minimize.

A good Christian concentrates on self,
Bible principles and nothing else.
Minding the tongue will always bring,
Christan friends and other good things.

Employ your energy on self-improvement,
and your tongue won't make a bad movement.
A rule of thumb is to engage the brain,
long before the words start to train.

(See James 3:1-13, Philipians 4:8 and I Peter 3-10)

## RICH MAN... POOR MAN

One has enough electric lights to turn night into day,
the other, the moon and stars to light the way.
One has an extra large yard of seventy feet or so,
the other, a front yard wherever you go.

One has a swimming pool in an oversized back yard,
the other, a lake that could be on a postcard.
One has a few shrubs and two or three scattered trees,
the other a forest and fields of flowers and bees.

One is boxed in by neighboring yards and traffic galore,
the other unlimited space when you exit the door.
One has a mansion for a house and no time to spare,
the other comfort and time to be aware.

One, to break even, has to pursue the almight buck,
the other can give thanks for his good luck.
One is caught up in material things that money can bring,
the other accepts life and necessary things.

In that ending struggle to find riches, what is lost,
when we find it, can we handle the cost?
What must we forfeit or give up to achieve that goal,
are we still Gods' and spiritually whole?

(A rich man sent his son to live with a middle class brother in the
country for a summer. When the boy returned, his dad asked how it
was to experince life on the other side of the track. The son said,
"Gee dad, it was swell! We slept outside at night without fear. And
we spent hours running over fields and through forests, swimming and
fishing in the lake in front of the house. We gathered up fruit from
the trees and vegetables from the fields. And you know, we had time
to go to church and give our thanks at dinner and before we went to
bed. Thanks, dad, for showing me how poor we are!")

12

## REFLECTION

Right now I wished I knew your problem better,
capable of saying things in verse or letter.
Providing wisdom that you could heed,
a little comfort when you are in need.

I can only listen and hurt a little inside,
show litle emotion and my feelings hide.
Stick to principles and not let myself bend,
and still be a very, very good friend.

I know what things plague your heart,
torn between two worlds that pierce like a dart.
Thoughts and emotions that never seem to settle,
shielding yourself as though you're made of metal.

I can understand 'cause I travel the same road,
sharing the world and its heavy load.
Think the things that you obviously do,
wish for this and that and other things, too.

So often we sit alone and ask ourselves why,
get caught up in thoughts to make us cry.
Wake up from another very troubled sleep,
still knowing things just had to keep.

The world certainly isn't the least bit fair,
with troubles that come beyond compare.
But isn't it nice to glance in a looking glass,
and see at least one person with some class?

## OUR BEST

A setting sun,
no one has won.
It comes and goes,
in spite of our woes.

Another day gone by,
for us to ask why.
Set aside human desire,
caught in a worldly mire.

Take that gift from Him,
before life goes dim.
Best to give, not to receive,
this is what we believe.

It's time to give back,
of that we don't lack.
Reach out to another,
gain a sister or a brother.

God has set the course,
there is no remorse.
Time to do our best,
before we fail the test.

# ONE OF A KIND

Look around and you will find,
God has made you one of a kind.
No matter what you think or do,
you won't improve on how you grew.

You don't need a tack in tongue or lip,
tatto's on arm, leg or hip.
Nor baggy clothes that are the trend,
just think of the message it sends.

Gang caps and jackets that are worn,
to only bring upon you lots of scorn.
Would it really make you feel proud,
to smoke, drink and hang around with that crowd?

I do not dare to speak the rest,
but all I want for me is the best.
I'm glad fools do what they do,
'cause it makes me different thru and thru.

## *A Human*

As an entity we are a comical sort,
from any angle, side or report.
Always changing things both near and far,
never satisfied as to who we are.

If we are white we strive to be darker,
If we are dark, to be white is a shocker.
If our hair is kinky or far too curly
and we can't straighten it out we get burly.

Oh, to have hair straight as a piece of string,
burnt roots and split ends permanents bring.
Changing the primary color or tint shade,
another decision has to be made.

We spend a lot of money to bring toilets indoors,
build large houses that are forty and some score.
Then work two jobs or more so we can afford
to camp and go to a potty that's outdoors!

We have to wonder with all this bother,
why God took the time as our Father;
To make us all unique and none the same,
if all these changes were going to be our game.

## DAY DREAMER

What a splendid time for all our day dreams,
the fun and games of life's schemes.
Imagine the worldly things you want to disappear,
ones that would fill everyone with cheer.

All those many things that don't amount to much,
struggles, disappointments and such.
Until they all pile on and on, one after the other,
with a tendency to smoother.

If we had the option and ability to pick and choose,
always win, win and never loose,
our lives would end up being down-right boring;
we'd spend most of our time snoring.

People that gather around us would all stand back,
thinking we were about to crack.
They definitely know we couldn't handle the pace,
of daily life without a race.

Struggles and disappointments that may befall
are necessary after all.
God uses these weaknesses to make us strong,
helping us learn right from wrong.

(See II Corinthians 1:3, 4:17, and 12:9;
Hebrews 2:10; Philippians 2:1-4; Acts 20:35;
I Peter 5:10; Galatians 6:2; and Romans 8:28-39)

## A Rainbow

In awe I looked out my window today,
to view the rainbow sent my way.
Gone were the pangs of sickness and pain,
the dreary days that came like rain.

The long days that I had to spend in bed,
wanting to do this and that instead.
Wishing and hoping to hold things in bay,
until I was up and about one day.

I thought about all my life's happy events,
all the achievements from good intents.
The roads we all must travel along the way,
with God's love with us every day.

When that journey seems difficult at best,
say a prayer and let God do the rest.
For I came to realize from God's majestic show,
it takes both sun and rain to make a rainbow.

## IN THE LIGHT

I know some day the Lord will explain,
what from life was to be our gain.
It certainly wasn't meant just to receive,
but give back from what we believe.

To accept what is life and all the morrow,
guided by Bible principles that we borrow.
Never to misuse the truth or in them mistrust,
follow that printed Word a definite must.

Each day touch another life here and there,
provide a positive influence everywhere.
Never hurry or worry and never complain,
understand those who pass the blame.

Accept each individual for who they are,
help them bring their life up to par.
Treat each person with sincere Christian love,
that is in the Bible and from above.

Remember to reach out to those who are in need,
with God's Word we all must heed.
Let the Lord guide us daily with His special care,
that is with us always, no matter where.

# RELATIONSHIPS...

## New Creation

The silence broken by the baby's first cry,
a husbands' anxiety released with a sigh.
The music to new parents that fills the room,
as new life comes forth from the womb.

At first glance the baby looks out of tune,
body out of proportion and skin like a prune.
Everyone still scurries to identify this shape,
comparison to family they all try to make.

"Look!" will say one, "It has your eyes and hair,"
another to remark of beauty beyond compare.
Assessing all features that make them so,
quick to pressure those who say they don't know.

The baby is struggling to adjust to the cold,
while being passed around for each to hold.
They look at us with eyes not seeing,
as we marvel at the creation of this little being.

We can't help but wonder what they are thinking,
as they view this new world with eyes unblinking.
From the quiet and comfort of their little nest,
to this noise, confusion and all the rest.

We also must wonder if given the choice,
would they stay where it was warm and moist?
We can only comfort them through life's first shock,
assure them that they come from very good stock.

In spite of genes from parents lent,
they'll grow into their own without repent.
They need only to follow the pattern that's set,
deeds parents accomplished and tasks they have met.

They have developed in months counting nine,
from a seed of love to one of a kind.
This little encounter is only the beginning,
but they have what it takes to come out winning.

# LOVE

Love can be defined in every way,
it can mean whatever you say.
We think it takes bells or chimes to ring,
and all sorts of other romantic things.

Women seek a knight on a horse of white,
men, a maiden fair glowing like sunlight.
We expect to see fireworks when lips meet,
pulses to quicken and hearts skip a beat.
You can get lost in many books of learning,
narrowing love to an area of concerning.

God has made it easy for us to define,
by understanding it's only a state of mind.
Not that important what love is, you see,
but what love isn't, if you want it to be.

Love is really a continuous and growing event,
a reflection of our being and every intent.
By treating each day with feelings of caring,
be it happiness or sorrow we are sharing.

Love bears, believes, hopes and endures all things,
that patience, understanding and kindness can bring.

(See I Corinthians 13:1-7)

# Courtship

Certainly no one has an exclusive corner on life,
on who will make the best husband or wife.
Wants and needs may get in the way,
and one or the other they may sway.

At best we can only stop and evaluate,
check our passion and put it on wait.
Think things out until feelings are certain,
placing all doubt behind the pasts' curtain.

Times' delay may seem like an eternity,
but decisions must be made with maturity.
Trusting in God with our faith focused above,
that life together will be from Christian love.

That is the essential and necessary soil,
for our roots in lifes' uncertain toil.
With that in place, nothing will dismay,
like an Oak, love will grow each day.

Everything must be from thoughtful caring,
in life together you will be sharing;
each giving the other the best at hand,
blending like the metal in the wedding band.

## FOR YOUR WEDDING

Marriage is not as difficult as they say,
just a minor adjustment each passing day.
Establishing values that will set you apart,
a compromise of love that is in your heart.

You must learn the essentials of "US,"
working together a necessary must!!
Forgetting the I and you, he and she,
blending together into that important "WE."

There will be times when all will seem lost,
tempers flare and others will boss.
Times and troubles that can tear you apart,
without understanding to give a new start.

When those troubles seem hard to bear,
remember always God's love you share.
Observe more closely your wedding band,
that life commitment on your left hand.

Note the continuous path around it's hollow,
no better direction for your love to follow.
Note also the metals in harmonious blend,
each from one the other to lend.

One metal provides a brilliant luster,
the other strength in it's atom cluster-
As your life must do as you continue together,
each of you giving your best to the other.

## Wedding Poem Explained

God, according to Genesis 2: 7, formed man from the dust of the ground, and breathed into his nostils the breath of life, and man became a living soul. Paul tells us in Thessalonians 2:8 what the soul is, "we were willing to have imparted unto you, not the gospel of God only, but also your own souls." Some translations render, "Our own souls" as "giving of ourselves."

Each of us is as distinct and unique as a snowflake and is like beach sand; part and particle of everything and everyone we come into contact with. We are a unique being confronting the rest of the world in a unique fashion. We are all different and we are meant to be. We all have a dinstinct personality with strengths and weaknesses. It is like a gold wedding band, which is highly prized for it's golden luster, but has not strength. Another metal is added to compensate and permit the gold to be formed into a strong ring that has no end in it's continuous circle. While it may loose some of its luster and shine over the years, the strength of the harmonious blend of metals never weakens.

In the book of Matthew 22:39, we read that the second greatest commandment is that "we should love our neighbors as ourselves." Paul, in Ephesians 5:25-33, brings that command in focus for the married couple. Verse 25 reads, "Husbands, love your wives as Christ also loved the church, and gave himself for it." Verse 28 reads, "So ought men to love their wives as their own bodies. He that loves his wife loves himself." Verse 29 reads, "...for no many ever hated his own flesh, but nourished and cherished it, even as the Lord the church." Verse 33 reads, "...nevertheless, let everyone in particular so love his wife even as himself, and the wife see that she has reverence for her husband."

Many critics decry that being yourself is selfish and self-centered. However, the concept of loving yourself is on the other side of the spectrum. While it flows from the center of our being, from within the innerself, it is not self-centered. To be oneself is a natural, human and universal objective. A person who values himself is much more likely to be able to do the same for others. When we are not sure who we are, we are uneasy. We try to find out what the other person would like us to say before we speak and what they would like us to do before we act.  When we are insecure, our relationships with others are governed not by what they need but by our needs.  Truly authentic people are there not only for themselves but for others.  No energies are wasted in protecting a shaky ego or in conflicts or deceits.

Striving for a perfect marriage is not easy.  In fact, it is a lifetime endeavor, and nobody ever makes it all the way.  It is a becoming rather than an ending, and people who experience success and happiness have both with them wherever they travel.  It becomes a way of life rather than a place to arrive.  The journey, a manner of traveling, rather than a destination.  In spite of temporary road blocks or diversions, instinctively keep you goals at hand to develop faith and confidence in each other and not fear;  strength and trust and not worry;  love and understanding and not anger.  Eliminate the word "argument" from your vocabulary and view them as a growing zone... an opportunity to learn and grow in a positive fashion.  Nothing in life is intended to be negative, it is only our perspective, our attitude and view point that makes it so.  To be angry or get angry is a God -given human emotion;  the sin is if we retain the anger and do not forgive.  Ephesians 4:26 says, "Be angry and sin not;  let not the sun go down on your wrath."  And something that will help us with positive thinking is Philippians 4:8, "Finally, brethren, whatsoever things are true, whatsoever things are honest (honorable), whatsoever things are just, pure, lovely, or good report;  if there be any virtue, and if there be any praise, think on these things."  Positive thinkers are focused dead center on solutions rather than problems.  When you have a conflict think first about what might bring about a resolution to the problem, rather than reacting with a "lets make trouble" posture.  One must work at avoiding conflicts, confrontations, name calling, complaining, manipulating, and instead, ask oneself, "What can I do to make this problem go away?!?"

*REMEMBER... LIVE EACH DAY TOGETHER AS THOUGH IT WAS YOUR LAST, AND REMEMBER THAT ONE DAY THIS WILL BE TRUE, AS NO ONE IS PROMISED A TOMORROW.*

## WHAT IS LIFE?

What is life without a little hope,
someone there to help you cope?
What is life without the rays of sun,
brought to you by a special one?

What is life and birds that sing,
without the harmony someone can bring?
What is life and natures folly,
without someone to make it jolly?

What is life and the blessings it can bring,
without someone to share in everything?
What in lifes' mornings can you share,
without someone being there?

What is life that God has provided,
if two loving hearts remain divided?
What is life when two don't walk together,
helping each other through lifes' stormy weather?

What is life that makes it so crazy,
when everyday is always so hazy?
It can be contributed to only one thing,
it lacks the sunshine each can bring.

# LIFE'S WALK

We have to bring many things together,
to help in storms we are to weather.
Those same stormy events can tear us apart,
when we don't speak from the heart.

With each gathering our personality and values,
from lifes' depths and all its shallows.
We are all different and that is God intended,
but points of view must be blended.

We must constantly build and strive to agree,
be it for two, four, or three.
Never lose focus of our God-given task,
we are in trouble if we have to ask.

Whatever the challenge presented before us,
the pros and cons we must discuss.
Sort out the negative from the positive terms,
and from them gain a lesson to learn.

We should never let personal feelings,
set up walls, floors or ceilings.
Keep an open forum for all our talks,
to guide us through lifes' walks.

## An Empty Nest

It is difficult when kids leave the nest,
join an adult world with the rest.
From birth each have been a special one,
and the reason things had to be done.

From first to last in your treasure chest,
no one singled out as the best.
From each we receive so many treasures,
that adds to our life's measures.

Photos will recall the days of by-gone years,
along with life's happiness' many tears.
Many memories will flash before our eyes,
as good is recalled and the bad left to die.

We gave them time and lots of love, you see,
taught right from wrong, and let them be.
Even when they were a naughty little bird,
we gave them each an encouraging word.

Parents have to provide a special love,
stern guidance and a gentle shove.
Teach not to speak wrong of one or the other,
remember they are sister or brother.

We often had to respond with quick reaction,
in twilight years after job satisfaction.
Sit down deep in that favorite easy chair,
knowing we gave them loving care.

When job is done as father and mother,
we can devote time to each other.
Enjoy together what life that may remain,
before our Lord lays down His claim.

## HAPPY ANNIVERSARY

Where have all the years gone so fast,
building memories in your past.
'Twas only yesterday vows from your heart,
proclaimed love till death do you part.
Now you should take the time to reflect,
good and bad memories for you to collect.
Look back and recall the kids' growing days,
things that made them different in every way.
The bruised elbows, knees and injured pride,
all the parental concern you had to hide.

Values you instilled so life would be easier,
challenges they met would be breezier.
Count the times you rattled the rafters,
also remember the hours of family laughter.
All your memories and much, much more,
are all behind history's door.
The future is always ahead of us and you,
the past a learning block for all we do.
Let us extend our blessing for your future life,
beyond this day as husband and wife.
In sickness and health, for better and for worse,
prayers are many but condensed in this verse.

May all the heavenly angles bring,
true feelings from the heart;
all of your life's happiness cling,
to the family you are a part.

May all the joy and sorrow
of daily life you share,
bring a happiness tomorrow,
built on kindness, love and care.

May the commitment on your left hand,
a confirmation of your bliss,
be it a small and simple gold band,
say more than a poem like this.

31

# PARENTS

So many things can cross our mind,
that make you stand out as one of a kind.
From the times you had to rattle the rafters,
to the many hours of family laughter.
The help you gave to make life worth living,
your thoughtfulness and constant giving.

The things you taught us kids to find,
values and joys of a worthwhile kind.
You demonstrated love by the example you set,
by deeds you've done and tasks you've met.

Remember and recall your growing days,
things that made us different in many ways.
The bruised elbow and injured pride,
all the parental concern you had to hide.
You shared some happiness and all our sorrow,
right there to say, "It will be better tomorrow."

We remember the times we had come to you,
for advice on what we had to do.
As we wander along our life's hard road,
with example received from our abode.
We will find many things to be thankful for,
as we realize who opened the door.

Years have passed and we travel still,
carrying out God's will.
We'll find our special niche in life,
in spite of all the daily strife.

# My Dog

They have rag-tag hide and oh-so-sad eyes,
chase balls and snap at flies;
an exciting life that's full of fun and joy,
that peaks over a new toy.

The pleasure a dog provides can't be measured,
just like any other God-given treasure.
Some attention, food, water and occasional treat;
no better friend will you ever meet.

An occasional woof, soft bark, or wagging tail,
is their way of sending e-mail.
When they respond to a few words from us,
it's from a superior love and trust.

No matter what you do, or where you go,
they greet you with the love they show.
They will remain faithful, loyal and true,
no matter what you say or do.

At fault or not, scold, howler, or yell all you can,
they'll apologize and lick your hand.
It takes a lot for their spirit to falter or break,
they'll stay faithful for goodness sake.

To strangers, they will snarl or bark as if to say,
"You there, best be on your way;
my owner placed this house in my trusting care,
so don't come in... no, don't you dare!"

# POEMS FOR
# SPECIAL
# PEOPLE...

# SANDY

Raised on a rural Westby farm,
along with it's Norwegian charm;
up early to do your farm chores,
then to school to learn some more.

Bused from school, when it was done,
more farm work beyond the setting sun.
From milking cows to feeding chickens,
not much time to be a little dickens.

After high school, a different job to mimic,
at Gundersen Pharmacy Clinic.
From there to the High School in Onalaska,
a long time there, we didn't ask ya.

Your life has always been complete,
with life tasks you had to meet.
A good marriage and many vacation trips,
to balance life's scales, when they may dip.

It was sad that Nelson had to leave,
but it was necessary we have to believe.
You cared for him without complaint,
wheeling him around like a little saint.

We all can learn from your plus years,
for each day, you deserve some cheers.
We know, and without any doubts,
you will handle all life's bouts.

## I'll Remember...

Each time I hear a motor boat roar,
see fog and hear a gentle knock at my door;
see a flock of Canadian geese in flight,
overhead both morning and night;
I'll remember...

The clang of boat chain and lock,
or hollow sound of a set line box;
wild ducks with their noisy report,
that you fed of every size and sort;
I'll remember...

Lookout and see a flat boat wake,
just like those you used to make;
set lining in spite of fog or mist,
it's only a part of a very long list;
I'll remember...

You've had an excellent run at life,
three loving kids, brother and wife.
I'll recall all those things,
that knowing you will bring;
This, no matter what else I do,
is my last birthday poem to you.
But, I'll remember...

## THE KID

The things one envision for a pack of six,
ole, coors, or bourbon and water as a mix.
But a boy at the start, and a boy at the end,
with four girls between, makes the odds bend.
Being the youngest hasn't been no big trick;
but at 35, "baby brother" just won't stick.
Even though, "I'm almost grown" you say,
to us, "The Kid" you'll always stay.

Artie, Denise, and your lovely wife Alice,
who make us at home in your little palace;
we want them to share in everyway,
all of our love on this special day.
We all decided to let you grow up,
and throw away your no-spill cup.
Replace it with a chain of 14 karat,
a reminder of your love as you wear it.

Each call from Arizona gives us a shudder,
we think, "Oh, no! Oh, no! Not another!"
We often wonder how much you can take,
or what other bones that you can break.
We would all like it if it were true,
away from the mine, and the black and blue.
Don't you agree, it's a little past time,
to join us and say, "To hell with the mine!"

Whatever  decision you care to make,
which job to do, to leave or take.
Above all else, we want you to know,
we are behind you in each lifes' throw.
Always remember our dear, dear brother,
the love we have, each for the other.
One that will not lessen or fade away,
but grows stronger with each passing day.


For the Alexander Family

38

# Danny

The death of your father early in life,
leaving six kids and a very young wife,
gave you accountability beyond compare,
adult responsibility you soon became aware.

It wasn't easy for all that we know,
with four sisters and a kid bro to grow.
To get on your way to deliver papers,
no time for a young man's capers.

Doing odd jobs to earn an extra buck,
left fun and games to others' good luck.

The things you gave up in childhood,
can't be replaced even if we could.
But we want you to know even still,
to have you as a brother was God's will.

Even though it's "fool" you always say,
it's said with love, in every way.
As we select a special time of year,
you must know our love doesn't stop here.
It carries back over so many things,
the sadness and gladness life brings.

Thankful now in our adults 'morrow,
for your strength and the love we had to borrow.
The time you gave to us, to one and another,
makes you the best, and one super brother!


For the Alexander Kids

## MIKE AND ALICE

Pack the flower and hit the road,
it's time to change your abode.
Move to here and move to there,
changes a job no matter where.

The city or town can't be a dud,
providing it has your favorite bud.
It seems you spend your life a-pack'n,
finding jobs to keep on cracking.

Always looking with a job sheet handy,
only to return back to Casa Grande.
It makes no matter where you are,
the call to you comes near and far.
"Ay Chihuahua aqua viene Alicia o Madre Mia,
caliente la placa, we'll roll some tortilla."

All these memories and much, much more,
are always behind the pasts' closed door.
You have to learn to adjust,
to live together; we all must.

And no matter what has been your test,
*HANG IN THERE AND GIVE IT YOUR BEST.*
Always look forward and you'll keep winning,
and make some time for sipp'n and grinning.

## PASSPORT BLUES

The mystery of a passport will unravel,
for the fun of foreign travel.
You will realize the questions and form
are not within the norm.

I asked them if they took American Express,
when I read about a Visa more or less.
I thought, glass or plastic, what would be worse,
when they told me I needed a picture first.

That just goes to show you how much I know,
I wonder if I should even go!
Ever so often I had to say, "Oh, me, oh my!
If things don't improve, I'll cry!"

I went to a regular photo shop that was near,
who advertised "Passport photos here."
The second or third sample caught my eye,
but they said it wouldn't fly.

It makes sense now the picture had to be of me,
for an easy to use ID.
That and my signature signed down below,
would aid me wherever I go.

Go here and there to get everything done,
trying hard to please everyone.
They talked about me- 'cause my ears burn,
I was confused at every turn.

I submitted my picture with paperwork norm,
received a passport in booklet form.
And it won't be long till I'll be on my way;
may even do it again, someday!

(Written for Eileen, who said I could probably even write a poem about
passports! While it took me back forty years to that confusion, I had to
add some humor to take away from the boredom!)

## DAVE'S HAT

Where, oh where is that darn cat,
that took off with Dave's hat?
We looked under siesta head,
Even underneath the bed.

Nowhere can we find,
that hat, one of a kind.
Filled with birthday joy,
even the little tinker toy.
A roll of paper with all the bends,
the kind you get from friends.

44

# SPECIAL
# EVENTS...

# THE GRADUATE

To celebrate this very special day-
but what to select from all those things
that won't swell heads or break angel wings?
To still convey the feeling of personal pride,
but will not the difficult times try to hide.
No point in giving false security,
letting you think life is all this purity.
Give a lot of praise without warning,
ease the shock of an adult's first morning.
Everything will change as it must,
new perspectives from dawn to dusk.

Childish thoughts may come back to mock,
as dreams and ideals succumb to future shock.
The longer days of making a living,
a little less taking and a lot more giving.
Learn from others, as we all have to do,
evaluate your values and start some anew.

As you brew your independence as an adult,
be mindful that others are part of the melt.
Always treat individuals as you would expect,
remember they also deserve your respect.
As you interface and ponder your life's test,
give it your all and ensure it's the best.
There will be no time to idle and waste,
you're in an adult world of hurry and haste.

Responsibilities and tasks started ages ago,
will now surround you from head to toe.
Soon will come the five days of working,
wishing again for school's laughing and smirking.
Decisions and lifestyle changes to make,
in a world that's not all diamond and jade.
The streets really aren't paved in gold,
life is what you make it, you'll behold.
Just keep on laughing and grinning-
we know you will come out winning!

### LUTEFISK AND LEFSE

The smell of Lutefisk cooking in the air,
  lefse folded and stacked with care.
Rutabaga boiling in a large cooking pan,
meatballs and potatoes mashed by hand.

Pies a plenty cooling on the window sill,
  homemade pickles, both sweet and dill.
Half a pound of melted butter for the fish,
  cranberry fluff and another side dish.

All the serving platters filled to the brim,
  folks sitting around with a silly grin.
Coffee, tea or milk, the standard drink;
  first helping gone quicker than a wink.

Some will take seconds of everything,
  to satisfy the appetite they bring.
Others will say, "One helping is enough!
I'm sorry, but I'm just not that tough!"

I'm the first to admit, it's an aquired taste;
but once you have it, nothing goes to waste.
Once or twice is enough for those who dare,
Lutefisk and lefse, a tasty Norwegian fare!

## CHRISTMAS

It's getting to be that time of year,
for Santa and his reindeer.
Presents and cheers delivered in an open sleigh,
for all to open on Christmas day.

There are bikes, cars, dolls, bears and trains,
those fancy wrapped, and some plain.
Children all snug and nestled in their bed,
their thanks given and blessings said.

Soon the sun will peek from over the hill,
highlighting frost on our window sill.
Snow, glistening and glowing in a brisk winter scene;
like a fairy tale, if you know what I mean.

The tree was trimmed and decorated just right,
with presents placed in the night.
Scrambling kids with eyes wide and faces aglow;
the present they got, they soon will know.

It really doesn't matter what each one got,
if they asked for it or not!
The aura that's present and fits like a glove,
is all the unity and family love.

# PATRIOTISM
## AND
## WAR...

## My America

Just take a good look at our majestic land,
ocean to ocean across prairie and mountain stand.
Our neighbors are varied and quite complete,
from the very poor to the prosperous elite.

Builders, doctors, farmers, machinists, and politicians fair,
factory workers, truckers and teachers beyond compare.
Civil servants, preacher, fire and policeman, dedicated all;
a ready and capable military to answer freedom's call.

Our strength not just in military power,
but in citizen response in any given hour.
We have come to fully understand,
what must be done for our freedom land.

The commitment to provide world peace,
when terrorists need only a short lease.
Often times we may want to complain,
things could be better and others to blame.

But no other nation on this earthly sphere,
can offer any more than we have here.
In counting each blade of grass or tall tree,
there isn't any other place I'd rather be.

# A VET

Some just can't appreciate a Vet like you;
all for America in everything you do.
But what can we expect from a protester's eye,
with their head inserted and butt to the sky?

Maybe those small-minded people without any class,
could see better with a belly button of glass.
On second thought, that wouldn't help to improve
their outlook on life or whatever they do.

They speak of love of country with concern and care,
do their own thing as though she wasn't there;
scurrying to manipulate self-serving results,
hiding behind words to cover up their faults.

In spite of education they fail to understand,
what has and must be done for our freedom land.
The personal commitment to maintain world peace,
when terrorists need only a very short lease.

Childish attitudes they will never let go,
emitting words that actions do not show.
Attempting to justify a self-serving dimension,
displaying an ignorance that needs no attention.

Trying to convince the world with every wail,
not knowing it's them that tips the scale.
Demoralizing service personnel with their events,
while helping terrorists in propaganda intents.

We can only pray that at least one day,
they'll realize what they had to say;
their signs and protesting yells
kill more people than any of our shells.

# *Fading Away*

They went through life without much ado,
    just a plain citizen like me and you.
    Yet, when there came a freedom call,
    They proudly arose and stood up tall.

Determined they went about our country's task,
    giving their best, and no one had to ask.
Accepted difficulties of sea, air, front and field,
    not once did selfishness cause them to yield.

As an American, we count them among our best,
    a definite notch or two above the rest.
Now they are fading sadly but proudly away,
    never to defend our country another day.

It is with daily numbers of a thousand or so,
    without any tribute as they go.
I think we should half mast our flags each day,
    just a dip salute;  it wouldn't have to stay.

(See I Timothy 2:1 and Romans 13:7)

Are not Christians suppossed to render
    honor to whom honor is due?

# PERSPECTIVE

It's no wonder we live in this state of affair,
with a country packed with those who don't care.
The majority too busy to give a darn,
unless it causes them personal harm.

Quick to criticize even the vets of Vietnam,
even those who died; they don't give a damn.
The question of course that I must ask,
why don't they go there with their task?

Instead they stay behind to shout even more,
in the safety of the country those vets died for!
It makes no sense when you think of it;
men die for others to speak their bit.

Maybe if they had seen it through a vet's eye,
villages burning and death staked to the sky.
A child's mangled and broken remains,
a mother laying nearby, reaching for same.

No sight on earth can begin to compare-
death looking out with a blank stare;
seeing nothing through those empty eyes,
not even their own smoke-filled skies.

Deaths' stare and wrinkled brow asking "Why?"
trying to reason why they had to die;
not knowing this was a Viet Cong day,
destined to die if they got in the way.

The old and very young who couldn't serve,
go what Cong considered they deserved.
Those women who were of the right age
were spared if they answered the page.

Behaved like Charlie thought she should
shared the virtues that were good.
Carried arms and joined in the fight,
took care of other needs in the night.

I can tell you from this Vets' heart,
what I've felt from the very start.
When I thought of a demonstrating duke,
my tummy wrenched and I nearly puked.

UnAmericanly I envy Charlies' frame of mind,
maybe his leadership is the only kind.
Keep those who are willing to serve,
giving protesters what they deserve.

55

# REFLECTIONS ON GOD...

# PATTERN

We pray our minds be opened wide
lest we be unlearned,
to recognize the destructive patterns
and then from them be turned.
To realize God's will from old through new
that the Bible tracks,
help us learn from Scriptures' truth
what our behavior lacks.

To teach us through God's precious Word
that we tarry not,
on evil things and worldly ways
that may be our lot.
Remind us daily of the destructive force
in the devils' lures;
the faith and hope in print we have
of preventions' cures.

The evil traps Satan works to set
lest we be aware;
all that which surely takes us
from God's loving care.
Help us study to earnestly learn
with all our mental might,
all the requirements for eternal life
by staying in God's light.

Let us learn from Noah when he built the ark;
Moses' instructions to build the tabernacle neither
missed the mark.
David did not follow the divine pattern and
Uriah lost his life.
The same price was paid by Ananias and Sapphira,
his devoted wife.

Let us learn from Revelation chapter three
verse five,
That we can be blotted from the book of life
and not be kept alive.
Let us also learn from what the Apostle Paul to Corinth he did say,
that even he had to practice what he taught.

# *I Am*

God is not a shell external,
but a Spirit that is eternal.
Not a specific creed or race,
black or white or any tonal face.

He is neither tall or short,
medium or any other report.
He told Moses, the Bible proclaims,
"I AM THAT I AM," at the bush of flames.

God provides a rainbow when rain is done,
our differences come from Noah's three sons.
Inter-marriages that still take place,
modifying yet another class or race.

The outer shell does not matter,
to think so makes it even sadder.
In His image He created you and me,
not external, but spiritual, you see.

Christ came to earth to teach,
looking like those He came to reach.
A definite part of a great plan,
to bring salvation across the land.

Christ built His Church on a rock- that's true;
He the Son of God; of the man Peter, me and you.
His kingdom neither here nor there, but within,
if the struggle of self we are to win.
No matter what foes may contrive,
He is real and very much alive.

(See Exodus 3:14; Genesis 1:27, 9:13 and 11:9;
Matthew 1:21 and 16:16-18; Luke 17:21 and Romans 7:15-23)

# THY KINGDOM COME

Christ taught us how to pray,
giving us the words to say.
"Thy kingdom come, thy will be done,
on earth as it is in Heaven" as one.

Many are unaware it is already here,
available to all that is clear.
Many say "It is here" or "It is there,"
others have no idea where.

His language is simple and just,
the kingdom is within us.
It is no building of great adorn,
just the shell in which we are born.

We are the church and truth in its meaning,
it is our understanding that needs a cleaning.
In spite of the Bible's clear direction,
we keep adding to our collection.

I wonder what it will finally take,
or explain for our souls sake.
To set aside the worldly bill of fare,
and focus on God's real concern and care.

(See Matthew 6:9-13 and 25:44;
and Luke 11:1-4 and 17:21)

60

# THE
# CHURCH...

## New Covenant

A new covenant was given to us,
laws put in our minds we can trust.
He also wrote them in our heart,
so from grace we would not depart.

To fulfill the law His Son came,
for our sins He took the blame.
Giving His life just had to be,
providing grace for you and me.

God closed the loop on sins' demise,
shut the door on Satans' first lies.
On truth Christ built a Church within,
to prevail against Satan and sin.

He consolidated the commandments in two,
making understanding easier for me and you.
Confirming His yoke was easy and His burden light,
making it easier to keep Him in our sight.

He also taught a model for us to pray,
providing a framework for each day.
We can talk to Him through group patter,
or personal e-mail for that matter.

(See Hebrews 8:10 and 10:16; Luke 17:21;
Matthew 6:6, 6:9-13, 16:16-18, and 22:36-40)

## WHY???

Why is it so difficult for us to conceive
of sin, if we do or do not believe?
Why must we change our direction in life,
forsake our Lord's work as man and wife?

Why can't we look deep inside to see who we are,
and bring our life in Christ up to par?
Why from worldly mistakes do we tend to hide,
if God truly joined that which no-one can divide?

Why can't we set pride and selfishness aside,
and in God's Word and grace alone abide?
Why can't we see brethren and familys' dismay,
over God's blessings that have gone astray?

Why did we get caught up in this way of doing,
unable to see that is is Satans' brewing?
Why didn't we stop the destructive mode,
and return God to our happy abode?

Why did we get caught in the devils' snare,
when the Bible teaches us to be aware?
Why is it we didn't heed that simple advice,
avoid worldly ways and all that vice?

Why do we continue to let evil tear us apart,
mocking God's Word that is inscribed in our heart?
Why do we compound the gamble with our salvation,
falsely justifying reasons to family and nation?

Why can't family and friends of any concerning
put a stop to this with all our learning?
Why in death will grief for us be more than most,
without forgiveness...
where we are going they cannot boast?!?!

## THE GOOD NEWS

If someone, either you or me,
counts the letters in "old," it is three.
The letters in "testament," one at a time,
will always add up to a total of nine.

To complete this little numerical rhyme,
side by side, that makes thirty-nine.
But wait, this is only half the book,
so let's pause and take another look.

Three times nine is twenty-seven,
the New Testament direct from heaven.
To show they are an excellent mix,
add them up for a total of sixty-six.

A complete library of countless facts,
that the story of salvation tracts.
Law, poetry, philosophy, psychology, history,
and most important of all,
solving God's Mystery.

## A Rainbow

In awe I looked out my window today,
to view the rainbow sent my way.
Gone were the pangs of sickness and pain,
the dreary days that came like rain.

The long days that I had to spend in bed,
wanting to do this and that instead.
Wishing and hoping to hold things in bay,
until I was up and about one day.

I thought about all my life's happy events,
all the achievements from good intents.
The roads we all must travel along the way,
with God's love with us every day.

When that journey seems difficult at best,
say a prayer and let God do the rest.
For I came to realize from God's majestic show,
it takes both sun and rain to make a rainbow.

# CHURCH
# LIFE...

# WELCOME

Please walk right up to where we stand,
we'd love to shake your hand!
Greet you with a warm and welcoming smile,
so glad you could stop by for a while.

We are all capable of reading the Bible the same,
misunderstanding it differently is the blame.
That is why its is so important and necessary for us
to investigate the key Scriptures and then discuss.

To us a Gospel ("good news") meeting is a big "to do,"
a guest speaker providing us with his view.
We are so very happy you could join us this week,
for the truth we came to seek.

With your comments we could be better learned,
and less of our Lords' concern.
Please plan to come back after this meeting is done,
so we can learn together, one on one.

### SINCE SIN ENTERED THE WORLD

Life is a funeral march from birth to grave,
a pathway worn thin by the humble and brave.
From birth it became man's destiny but to die,
to the music of a widows' sigh or an orphans' cry.

A river of tears have been shed every day,
since sin entered this world of ours to stay.
And if those tears flowed to just one spot,
it would form an ocean deeper than any we've got.

And if the groans uttered since the beginning,
accounting in total for all of the sinning,
were gathered into one volume of sound,
the thunder in the sky would split the ground.

And if the broken hearts from Eden until now,
could be stacked up high somehow,
they would top any current mountain tall,
and sin it would be that had caused it all!

(Author's note: While sin coming into the world started all of our
difficulties, God is faithful and we will not encounter anything uncommon to man. In addition, this life is but a twinkle in the eye compared
to eternity and, by faith, eternity is what we have to look forward to.)

# CHURCH OF CHRIST

We are just ordinary folks in our Christian youth,
searching Scriptures for the truth.
Speaking only who, what, why and where the Bible speaks,
never adding or subtracting perks or peaks.

Our Lord and Creator have gone to many different extremes,
revealing the mystery of redemption's scheme.
From the Old Testament throughout the Testament New,
the mystery is disclosed for me and you.

It is always our study objective and heartfelt goal,
to understand salvation as a whole.
Follow the covenant words put in our hearts and mind,
that was part of God's design.

Our infrastructure goes back to the very beginning,
when Christ gave His life for mans' sinning.
Our name, upon the Rock (truth) provided Peter and crew,
He the Son of God;  from man, Peter and you.

To prevail and stand forever against Satan and sin,
His kingdom built from within.
We stress the development of that inner being,
learning from Scriptures we are seeing.

Striving to learn Christian behavior the Bible tracks,
improving in areas that we lack.
We are the Church and this building a meeting place,
to expand Christ's foundation face to face.

## ONCE SAVED, ALWAYS SAVED

Many will attempt to tell you the Scriptures surmise,
all you really need is to be baptized.
Others will tell you that it only takes believing,
but you know they have to be deceiving.
Another group, "it's faith only," they will proclaim,
and lead you to damnation without shame.
Still others say it's "works only" that you can bet,
like you are repaying some unknown debt.
Not everyone shall enter the kingdom of heaven,
for many will never purge out the leaven.
Especially those who depend on false triviality,
and forsake God's perfect law of liberty.


It's not the false teachers of noted fame,
who should be given total blame.
"What is the price of a Bible?" you should ask,
to read and study our responsibility and task.
There are far too many Scriptures that you can read,
inspired teachings that you must heed.
For the pathway is narrow with a straight gate,
built on love and not worldly things or hate.
The second epistle of John in his verse nine,
sums it up in a very short time.
Jesus himself said His yoke was easy and His burden was light,
so it can't be that hard to stay in His sight.

(continued)

## One Saved, Always Saved (con't)

The Lord's hand is not shortened that it cannot save,
as long as we walk in the doctrine and behave.
Neither is His ear heavy that it cannot hear,
if the inspired Word we do no jeer...

Iniquities will separate between God and you,
be mindful of them in whatever you do.
Sin will hide His face and He will not hear,
that is what we must understand and keep clear.
Christ will not know us if we work in the dark;
He'll ask us to depart from Him for missing the mark.
We are asked to set our affections on things above,
work not in darkness nor be caught up in worldly love.
There is but one body, one spirit and one calling,
one Lord, one faith, one baptism to keep us from falling.
One God and Father of all, who is above all,
and grace through the gift of Christ to answer our call.

See Scripture references of...

Matthew 7:13 and 21;  I Corinthians 5:7 and 8;
James 1:25;  John 2:10-15;  II John 8 and 9;
Galatians 2:4 and 5;  and II Timothy 3:16

# REFLECTIONS
## ON THE
# END OF LIFE...

# HOLD YOUR FORK

After enjoying a picnic or potluck meal,
delicious desserts are part of the deal.
When they gather dinner dishes you can bet,
you keep your fork for the best yet.

Just think of your life as kin to that dinner,
mortal death as dessert for a winner.
Then picture yourself in a coffin if you will,
fork in hand as you lie there still.

If we would pass from this earth's land,
with a fork placed in our hand,
it would be a definite reminder to some,
the best for us is yet to come.

Remembering, when it is time to leave,
the fork will help us not to grieve.
The Scriptures confirm to both me and you,
the best yet for us is still our due.

Partake of unleavened bread and fruit of the vine,
God's saving grace that is yours and mine.
Let bottled-up life worries and troubles remain uncorked,
and always hold on to God's dessert fork.

# BACKGROUND ON "HOLD YOUR FORK"

This poem is based on the August 12, 2000 Ann Landers column "Keep Your Fork" as it appeared in the La Crosse Tribune in La Crosse, WI. A woman was diagnosed with a terminal illness and given three months to live. She asked her pastor to come to her house to discuss her final wishes. She told him which songs she wanted sung at her funeral, what Scriptures to read, and which outfit she wanted to be buried in. Then she said, "One more thing... I want to be buried with a fork in my hand."

The pastor was suprised. The woman explained, "In all my years of attending church socials and potluck dinners, I remember that when the dishes of the main course were being cleared, someone would inevitably lean over and say, "Keep your fork." It was my favorite time, because I knew something better was coming, like a velvety chocolate cake or deep-dish apple pie- something wonderful! So, I want people to see me there in that casket with a fork in my hand and wonder, "What's with the fork?" Then, I want you to tell them, "Keep your fork, because the best is yet to come.""

At the funeral, when people asked the pastor why she was holding a fork, he told them of the conversation that he'd had with the woman before she died. He said he could not stop thinking about that fork, and knew they probably would not be able to stop thinking about it, either. He was right. So, keep your fork, for the best is yet to come!

## DIAGNOSIS

When my x-ray came back all marked,
I knew the next talk would not be a lark.
The doctor could barely look me in the eye,
to tell me I had a one percent chance to survive.

It didn't catch me off guard or make me blue,
as a Christian he didn't tell me anything new.
We all have to face mortal death day by day,
It is a definite fact of life- we can't stay.

It is just a simple matter of how or when,
cause the end results we cannot bend.
The statistics of one in a hundred were mine,
so the doctor and I prayed for those ninety-nine.

In my mind the doctor was as wrong as can be,
I wasn't going to die; no, not me!
Someday I will leave this place called Earth,
and take my place with heavenly mirth.

While it may be sad for those left here,
as I leave, I'll click my heels and cheer.
My heart goes out to those who can't watch me die;
just don't look in a mirror unless you can lie.

We are all destined to leave this earthly sphere,
disconnect from normal activities here.
But it's far, far from being the end,
for life eternal will just begin.

(Author's note: I held this poem back for eight years until prompted
to share my positive attitude with others for encouragement. If you understand
the point of this poem, you will discover that nothing changes when you are
terminal. We are given that status the day we are born. From that day on
it is just a matter of how and when. And as I told many spouses of the
terminally ill I have talked with, "If you have trouble watching someone die
day by day, don't look in the mirror at yourself, because you are in that
catagory as well." When someone is terminal, nothing changes. From birth on,
we all die day by day. Remember that when you visit someone. Be natural, smile
and joke as you normally do; they will be better for it, and so will you!)

76

## OOP'S

With only a one percent chance for survival,
greed wrung it's hands on my arrival.
In my ignorance I didn't listen to the VA,
gave into a local to do it their way.

At the time, it was normally the general thought,
remove the cancer, anything else is naught.
If everything went as it should have been done,
I would have been a blessed one.

It is fairly obvious I was "training ground"
for someone not long around.
Clumsy hands messed up the cancer removed,
lung taken out, only a portion approved.

Broken ribs never healed, left vocal cord was cut,
which left a sinking feeling in my gut.
My left shoulder blade has a mind of it's own,
over-radiation softened all of my bones.

I could no longer teach, do hobbies, hunt or fish,
clean house or cook my favorite dish.
Nor complete wood-working projects that I had started;
the ability to repair or build also departed.

Still, having ten years of being cancer free,
in spite of pain, filled me with glee.
But now, much to everyone's suprise and dismay,
Cancer in the other lung showed up to stay.

The Apostle Paul said it far better than I,
as I contemplate the fact that I die.
I found myself also caught between the two,
to join Christ or to stay here with you?

I do know what is ahead is definitely my gain,
greed took my options, I can't remain.
If you are afraid to laugh or look me in the eye,
galnce in a mirror at someone else who will die.

We all have to live our life in this day we borrow,
for no one is promised another tomorrow.
To God, I humbly give thanks for so many things,
As the Christian love knowing each of you brings.

# GROWING OLD

Each day I get a little more forgetful as I grow old,
"Confused and a little mixed up" is what I have been told!
Word association didn't work returning your phone call,
I forgot my objective as I walked down the hall.
Instead of picking up and dialing the kitchen phone,
I went to the freezer and got an ice cream cone!

I get confused when I find myself stopped near stairs;
was I going up, or coming down from there?
With pantry or icebox door open, my mind fills with doubt,
did I just put food away, or come to get some out?
I often find myself standing in the dark scratching my head,
and wonder if I am getting up or just going to bed?

Often when I call my family to dinner, all filled with pride,
the table is set, but where is the food? Did it hide?
I then call for pizza delivery for this family of mine,
but did I give the right address so it will arrive on time?
Even now, as I shake your hand and look you in the eye,
I don't know if I should say "hello" or "goodbye!"

From birth to 40 we live each day as though it's the first of the rest,
and after 65 each may be our last, so we give it our best.
At the age that I am at, it seems that I subscribe alternately to each,
so I don't know if I am coming or going- isn't that a peach!?!?

## IF ONLY

We were open and tried to be a good friend,
gave and gave, always the one to bend.
Giving support;  writing, calling, or just dropping by,
holding folks up when they needed a good cry.

Standing in the shadows and sharing the blame,
never putting down or causing shame.
Praying when our time came, life will Balance things out,
and pay back would come about.

We then came to know what it is like to be an old shoe,
cast aside;  ignored no matter what we do.
We try to be obvious without flashing lights glare,
while folks carry on like we aren't there.

The fight is gone and it seems no matter how hard we try,
depression lingers and controls by and by.
Every day we wake, filled with hours that are lonely,
wondering what it would be like, If only!

(Author's note:   Have you ever gone to a convalescence home to
visit a friend or relative?  While there, did you notice all of the
residents who just never seem to have visitors?  Ever look into those
haunting eyes and wonder what they must be thinking?  Or, did you
ever see a quick twinkle light up those sad eyes if you wave to them?
I expect this poem speaks for them!)

# TRAGEDY

Life provides many avenues of travel,
a lot of mystery to unravel.
Many will cause our faith to stumble,
if we don't sort out the rubble.

If, in a tragedy, some live and some die,
it's all right to wonder "Why?"
But it is certainly ridiculous to think or say,
God made it happen that way.

To save some and destroy the rest,
is not God or His test.
He doesn't choose or separate anyone,
nor His will, that it be done.

His love and grace for us is always at a peak,
providing strength when we are weak.
If you escape mortal death with another chance,
make the most of it without a second glance.

(See Matthew 5:45;  Ephesians 6:9;  James 2:1;
Colosians 3:25;  I Peter 1:17;  and Acts 10:34)

(Author's note:   Often, when a plane or train crashes, someone will survive
or miss the connection and explain, "It was God's intervention." Or, "By
the grace of God I was spared," or "God was looking out for me or them."
While faith is a good thing to have and hold on to, I think it is a stretch to
believe that one or two were spared and God let the rest parish.  Events
happen in our life that are sometimes unexplainable;  mysteries that escape
comprehension.  But, they are just that.  God neither wants or deserves the
negative credit or blame!)

# PAIN

Lord, take this mountain from their view,
it won't move no matter what they do.
They have tried and tried to overcome the pain,
but day after day they make no gain.

Lord, they try to be a good Christian example,
in life's encounters we all must sample.
Willing to carry more than their share,
of grief, pain and life's daily despair.

Now they pray each day to wake and see,
health back to normal as normal can be.
But each sunrise brings no change of pace,
and still all the pain they have to face.

Forgive them for what has been done and left undone,
Overlook the race(s) they ran and never won.
We pray, Oh Lord, if all this pain can't be put away,
take them home before the end of this day.

(Author's note: I am sure we have all encountered someone
described in this poem. I know that for me, the hardest prayer I
made was for my own father. He had a tumor that was so large it
was breaking through his skin, and he was in so much pain that
he couldn't move. I thank God that the medical profession has
finally recognized drug addiction is secondary to comfort for the
dying. Thankfully, few patients go through that much discom-
fort anymore.)

## A WALK

Oh, what a pleasure to walk down the street,
   wave at all the good folks you meet.
See a happy-go-lucky smile on a strangers' face,
   laughing and merriment in every place.

The stress and fast pace of life all in the past,
   a genuine peace and calm at long last.
Struggles and difficulties you encounter each day,
   vague as though they never happened anyway.

I look down from above at my walled enclosure,
   and the folks trying to maintain composure.
I am glad to see so many that I can readily recognize,
from my neighbors, friends, and church they comprise.

The sensuous smell of fresh cut flowers fills the room,
   a Spiritual aura to spell the gloom.
Soon my stroll will be over and rays of light will fade,
   as the lid is closed and the latch made.

Please, don't you feel the least bit sad or even cry,
   I'm on my way to meet my Lord in the sky.
I am looking forward to that promise He made to you and me,
   and I'll be there to greet you, just wait and see!

(Author's note: It is getting to be commonplace to pick up a
newspaper, listen to the TV or the radio, and learn of someone
experiencing an "out of body" experience. Some claim to have
come back from the dead. This poem is a look at that experience.
I don't know if they are true or even possible. I do know that I
have prayed that God would leave me here for a short time so I
could see the world as other folks; that is, through eyes that are
not colorblind.)

# THAT DASH

As we look at that cold gray stone,
etched and shaped by a carvers hone;
we see the name of a loved one or two,
someone who meant a lot to me or you.

Beneath the name are the dates of a brief life,
with no mention of accomplishments or strife.
Those ordeals are contained as they are known,
in that dash between the dates that are shown.

All that was accomplished of any merit,
are also held there in fourteen karat.
The growing years, work and social field,
are also hidden in that dashes' shield.

It takes only a second or two and no more,
to read the name, date and credit score.
But if you are in a hurry my friend,
don't read the dash, 'cause it doesn't end.

(Author's note: We come into this world as a unique individual.
Our personalities develop from everyone and everything we
come into contact with. As we gather, we also impart our
distinctive traits to others around us. Hence, when we leave
this earthly sphere, we leave behind our footprints in the sands
of time.)

## Scriptures Referred to in
## Life's Dark Door

### Genesis 2:4 -7

"(4) These are the generations of the heavens and the earth when they were created.  In the day that the Lord God made the earth and the heavens, (5) when no plant of the field was yet in the earth and no herb of the field had yet sprung up- for the Lord God had not caused it to rain upon the earth, and there was no man to till the ground; (6) but a mist went up from the earth and watered the whole face of the ground- (7) then the Lord God formed man of dust from the ground, and breathed into his nostrils the breath of life;  and man became a living being."

### Ecclesiastes 3:17- 22

"(17) I said in my heart, God will judge the righteous and the wicked, for He has appointed a time for every matter, and for every work. (18) I said in my heart with regard to the sons of men that God is testing them to show them that they are but beasts.  (19) For the fate of the sons of men and the fate of beasts is the same;  as one dies, so dies the other.  They all have the same breath, and man has no advantage over the beasts;  for all is vanity. (20) All go to one place;  all are from the dust, and all turn to dust again. (21)  Who knows whether the spirit of man goes upward and the spirit of the beast goes down to the earth?  (22) So I saw that there is nothing better than that a man should enjoy his work, for that is his lot;  who can bring him to see what will be after him?"

### I Corinthians 15:35,36,38-40,42

"(35) But some one will ask, "How are the dead raised?  With what kind of body do they come?"  (36) You foolish man!  What you sow does not come to life unless it dies.  (38) But God gives it a body as He has chosen, and to each kind of seed its own body.  (39) For not all flesh is alike, but there is one kind for men, another for animals, another for birds, and another for fish. (40) There are celestial bodies and there are terrestrial bodies; but the glory of the celestial is one, and the glory of the terrestrial is another. (42)  So it is with the resurrection of the dead.  What is sown is perishable, what is raised is imperishable."

# LIFE'S DARK DOOR

We must sadly look at life's dark door,
remember things that can be no more.
Grieve with those who are heavy hearted,
cry from thoughts that a loved one has departed.

Let's stop to realize and really see,
an end to this life just has to be.
But are they really gone we must ask,
or only terminating their earthly tasks?

We can find some gladness in our sorrow,
if we remember that promise for tomorrow.
No longer with us in that we can trust,
pray God will raise them from the dust.

Remove them from their frayed body of earth,
with an indestructible one of heavenly mirth.
Grant them an eternity of heavenly life,
free from all this worldly strife.

May we have no fear of salvation's great atone,
pray across Jordan we will not travel alone.
For in reality we can only hope and pray,
for God's grace to join them again one day.

(Scriptures on page Eighty-four are quoted from
the Revised Standard Version.)

We read in Genesis 2:7 that God formed man from the dust of the ground and breathed into his nostrils the breath of life and man became a living soul. Please note, God did not give man a soul, but rather, he BECAME one. Paul defines the soul for us in Thessalonians 2:8, "we were willing to have imparted unto you, not the gospel of God only, but also our own souls." Some translations render, "our own souls" as "giving of ourselves."

Each of us is as distinct and unique as a snowflake, and like beach sand, part and particle of everything and everyone we come into contact with. We are all different and are meant to be! However, just as we pick up or "gather" our personality as we go through life, we also impact or impart our personality onto others as we travel life's highway. Family traits are the strongest of these subtle pebbles, and one can look at a sister or a brother and readily see the mother or father.

A good example of this can be understood by observing a light bulb. The bulb is the body and when electricity ("breath of life") is applied, the bulb emits light ("soul"). Thus we have taken two separate things and created a third. That light, while burning, influences everything it comes into contact with. It provides diretion, points out our way, helps things grow, etc. Should the light go out, all of the good things still continue and we can view its presence in all of the objects it has touched. Just as God intended and confirms in Ecclesiastes 3:20, "all go unto one place; all are of the dust, and all turn to dust again," and in verse twenty-one, "who knoweth the Spirit of man that goeth upward."

(Continued on next page...)

## *Life's Dark Door Explained (Con't)*

In I Corinthians 15:35 a question is noted, "but some man will say, "How are the dead rasied up? And with what body do they come?"" Verses thirty-six through forty-one explain the various aspects of celestial and terrestrial bodies and the summary is in the remaining verse, the heart of which is in verse forty-two, "so also is the resureection of the dead. It is sown in corruption and it is raised in incorruption." In verse forty-four we read, "It is sown a natural body; it is raised a spiritual body. There is a natural body, and there is a spiritual body."

In the book of Luke 16:19-31, we can read the story of Lazarus (a poor beggar, with sores licked by the dogs and fed with crumbs) and the rich man. In this account, they both died. While the beggar was carried by angels into Abraham's bosom, the rich man woke up in torment in hell. He pleaded for mercy and for Lazarus to be sent, that he might dip his fingers in the water, and cool his tongue. When Abraham refused, the rich man asked to return to his father's house to warn his brothers so that they could avoid this place of torment. We can glem from this story that after our earthly death we are aware of those we leave behind. Also, we can gleam that those who procede us in death will be waiting for us.

# POEMS
# FOR FUN!

## LIFE HAPPENS

One day I went out for a very short winter walk,
    stopped on a hill with my neighbor to talk.
Children were all around and yelling with glee;
    "Push me, push me" was their anxious plea.

I slipped and went down the hill on my keister,
    kids asking, "Where's your sled, mister?"
    I told them that I had a wallet tri-fold,
    I hope the binding and stitching will hold!

I extended my hands and arms out on each side,
    trying desperately to control this wild slide.
Even tried to dig in with both hands and boot heels;
    my speed just increased like I was on wheels.

The brass buttons on my pockets certainly didn't help,
    they were getting warm and I was about to yelp.
Quickly realizing my embarrassment I couldn't hide,
    it was best to just lay back and enjoy the ride!

(See I Corinthians 10:13;  II Corinthians 4:17-18;
    Philippians 3:13, 4:8, and 4:11-13)

(Author's note:  Ever so often we travel on life's highway and get blind
sided by an icy spot.  And it seems, no matter what we do, those
hindrances get out of control.  Life happens, and all we can do is set our
sight on the positive and learn from our experiences.)

## RHUBARB PIE

The smell of a fresh baked rhubarb pie
is enough to make your tummy cry!
With a tasty and layered crust,
it just doesn't seem just!

Almost a shame to cut that delicate skin,
hand trembling so our taste buds can win.
It's like destroying a priceless piece of art,
first cutting across, then slicing apart.

Our taste buds will yell with surprise,
confirming what we had surmised;
it will be the best we've ever tasted,
nary a crumb of it will be wasted!

## FLEET RESERVE TRANSFER

A point in time has come in my life,
to set aside this Navy strife.
A time to forget that troublesome hertz,
and let civilian life become the nerts.
A time to forget those across that big bay,
and the shipboard life to take us that way.

On Twenty October, Nineteen-Seventy-Nine,
help me celebrate, if you will be so kind.
Plan to start at the hour of four,
walk on in; don't knock at the door.
Food will be provided, not a gourmet delight,
brew and punch and something without that bite.

Take Federal Boulevard from College, or 94 where they meet,
then turn to 6532 Mallard; it is an extra wide street.
Immediately up a hill, in a southern direction,
the equivalent of four blocks from that intersection.
It's the house on the left, at the bottom of the dip,
the first in line so it can't give you the slip.

The October air is chilly, when the sun starts to dim,
but a pool is available, if you like to swim.
Bring a bathrobe or jacket and a towel or two,
to prevent you from turning a certain shade of blue.
We hope to socialize and enjoy some idle chatter,
discuss the weather and whatever else may matter.
No matter what else, it won't be a big ado,
unless I can share this special day with you.


Given for Blaine R. Thorson
RMCM, USN, RET


92

## UFF DA

There is nothing like Norwegian Pride,
an ethnic group with nothing to hide.
They laugh and joke about each other,
even suggest they're born without a mother.

No topic or characteristic is out of bounds,
when jokes start to make their rounds.
Lena and Ole seem to play the lead role,
living in an outhouse with half a hole.

Renting from Lars that old outhouse,
and to show you that he is not a louse,
he will find someone who is in need,
and rent that basement to a Swede.

Even Lars and Ole are a sporting pair;
hunting life isn't the least bit fair.
Throwing a dog in the air didn't bring 'em luck,
it kept coming back down without a duck.

In Spring they planted 50 pounds of bird seed,
instead of birds, they got a bunch of weeds.
Never discouraaged by the life that goes by,
being Norwegian is pie in the sky.

# P

Brrrrrrrr, it is so ca, ca, ca cold,
I won't be able to hold...
Oh me, oh my, oh my, oh me!
I gotta go, I gotta go P!


It's night, it's night, it's night,
where, oh, where is my uplight?
But I don't dare to hurry, hurry;
I gotta worry, worry, worry.


I have no chance at all to make it,
if the hallway isn't lit.
Oh gee, oh gee, now I'm getting all wet,
not even half way there yet!


I woke up much to my surprise,
on the patio at sunrise.
I wasn't really in any great pain;
it was just me sleeping in the rain!


(Author's note: Isn't it amazing how dreams seem to manifest
themselves?  Events or fears that lurk in the shadows of our minds
appear from nowhere.  Things we never consider in our waking
hours and yet are prevalent as we sleep!)

# PART TWO

---

# ESSAYS

"If we walk in the light, as God is in the light, we have fellowship with one another, and the blood of Jesus Christ His Son will cleanse us from all sin." (I John 1:7). Doesn't that verse lend credence to a prayerful song we sing, "Just A Closer Walk With Thee"? The words, "In the beginning" are beautiful opening words in the Bible, and are an appropriate start for our walk in the light. In the beginning, we are just a thought, an idea, a plan, in the minds of our parents, much like the creation of the world must have been for God. A creation from love, for love, and endured by love, not so much removed from what is reflected on in the Bible. "For God so loved the world, that He gave His only begotten Son, what whoso-ever believeth in Him shall not perish, but shall have everlasting life." (John 3:16) It is significant to note that, in spite of our contrary nature, the pain and disap-pointment we generate, not to mention our sinful ways, "He so loved us." That four-word phrase is certainly a measure of the patience accorded mankind since the beginning of time.

Our requirement, and equally encompassing commit-ment, is summarized in the greatest commandment: "You should love the Lord your God with all your heart, and with all your soul, and with all your mind. Which is the first and most important; and the second is like it- You should love your neighbor as yourself. On these two commandments hang all the law and the prophets." (Matthew 22:37-40) Please note that in verse forty it is telling us that the ten commandments and all of the rules set forth by the prophets are summarized in these two commandments.

The very foundation of your walk in the light must begin with the understanding of these two commandments. It is essential to note that the first and most important commandment does not set up a pecking order as proposed by mankind (I am thinking of "God, country, then family"), but rather it requires that you take God with you wherever you go and in whatever you do. (See Colossians 3:17 and 23 and Ephesians 6:6 and 7) The second commandment embodies the golden rule, "do unto others as you would want them to do to you," that we read in Matthew 7:12. Both of these Christian commandments require the development of self-disciple, maturing of the inner person, and constant work on the largest room in the world: that of the "room for improvement." Your appreciation of the new covenant will increase as you contrast the verbosity of the Law of Moses from the Old Testament and the expostulative faith of the New Testament. In essence, the commandments and related laws have matured through the use of our intellectual ability, coupled with common sense. (See Romans 13:9 and II John verse 9). You will need the forgiving power of Christ in your daily life. (I John 1:8)

Contrary to what some religious leaders have said, you cannot buy your way into Heaven. Nor will any amount of money contributed to shrines, left to churches or put toward building funds erase one sin from your book of life or gain you better living quarters in Heaven. Doing the will of God is the only required "entrance fee." (See John 14:2 and 6 and Matthew 7:21) God does love a cheerful giver and we should always contribute when and what we can afford, as read in II Corinthians 9:7. But, our offerings should always be from a grateful and loving heart without expectations of special considerations and rewards.

In the beginning, we were set out to be different, unique, and having no comparison. We were destined to travel on our own life highway; a path that no one else has ever traveled and never will. No one else will ever experience life in quite the same way and manner that you will! No one else will ever respond to life in quite the same way and manner that you do, either! We can conclude, therefore, that the study of one's self is undoubtably the hardest, yet the most important, mission a person can accomplish. To know oneself is truly the foundation of all knowledge. That knowledge is an integral trait in great leaders and successful people. An individual with well-structured self-discipline, who can respect and value themselves, are more likely to respond to another in kind. (See Philipians 2:3 and 4) Moreover, they will possess an inner strength that radiates self-confidence and the courage of their convictions. (See I Peter 2:20) They are reliable, instinctively honest, and never restrain their ethical position with an unjust compromise. (See Colossians 3:17 and 23)

On the other hand, individuals who lack self-assurance, self-control and the mettle to stand behind their convictions are habitually anxious in any social environment. (See James 1:5 and 6) In spite of positive influences and encouragement, they will have a tendency to return to old behavior patterns when left to their own devices. (See II Peter 2:22) When an individual is not sure who they are or what they represent, they will attempt to learn what the other person would like them to say before they contribute to a conversation. Or, they will try to figure out what others' expectations are before they get involved. This demeanor is an excellent checkpoint for us.

If our relationships and responses to others are controlled by our own selfish needs, we will acquire a reputation for being wishy-washy for our inconsistency of reslove. (See James 1:8)

Instead of wasting a lot of money, time and effort putting out individual branches of a fire, wouldn't it make more sense to put out the main fire or at least get it back under control?!? No matter what you think, or what you perceive is wrong with society, is it our fault. We have lost control. We let a few people, who I'm sure think they did or are doing the right thing, tell us how to raise our children. We have become quick to tell our children that they have rights, but fail to explain how those rights have to be earned. More important, with those rights come responsibility and accountability! We let one group strip away parental and teacher disciplining power, and another group reduces schooltime patriotic activities to reviewing in a textbook. At the same time, evolution (theories having to do with man developing from fish and monkeys) and the Big Bang theory are being taught in our schools without the counterbalance of the creation theory. Also, non-believers are challenging religious artifacts on public display in the courts. It doesn't seem to bother them that the money they spend, or horde, has "In God we trust" printed and stamped on it. Often small groups of atheists are accomplishing things because the majority group of theists are letting the atheists do these things! They know full well what is written in the U.S. Constitution and the intention of it's writers. They achieve goals relying on public ignorance and passiveness to incite support. (See Acts 19: 32) If our liberal Supreme Court lacks common sense, then we need to petition the lawmakers (Congress) to write specific amendments putting these essential American moral growth elements back into the classroom.

If you plotted the past 40 years or so on a chart, your would readily see that while teen incidents have increased, attendance in church, participation in Girl and Boy Scouts and other positive activities have decreased. Get involved yourself! I can tell you from my own experience that you will never experience a greater joy or pride than a one-on-one enounter with your child in one of these activities. We only have a small window of opportunity to set in place behavior that will be with our kids the rest of their lives. With our hectic schedules, what better minimal time opportunity is available than a couple hours a week with our children in Church and in Bible study? "Grow up a child in the way he must go, and when they grow up they will not depart from it." (See Proverbs 22:6) When we create a positiv environment for our children, we are building for the future. Your influence will reach far beyond your small circle. It molds not only your children, but also countless friends they will come into contact with during their lifetime. Children need discipline, acceptance, and a sense of belonging to develop self-discipline. They need structure, rules, attention with praise and not a constant nipping, nagging or scolding. (See Ephesians 6:4) Parent were meant to guide, not to crush, a child's individual ideas and initiative. Every person, even a child, is entitled to his or her own point of view. While children should never become mere pawns in the hands of parents, schoolteachers, or anyone else, they need to understand respect for parents and other adults. (See Colossians 3:21) Above all, we must exercise common sense and caution in what we convey to them. For example, if we make them apologize when they do something wrong, we have to be careful that they are not learning they can do anything they want, as long as they apologize. We all need help, but other's can't do it for us, lest we end up like the mothers of Lee Harvey Oswald or Sirhan Sirhan when they cried out that "others were responsible!" If these words from 1963 are beyond your pesonal recall, then think instead of the recent school bombings or random destructive gang activities that occur in so many neighborhoods.

Are there any magic answers for raising a child in today's world? Do we have the time to sort through the preponderance of conflicting information written on this subject? Remember, "there is nothing new under the sun." I can only conclude that the Bible worked for our parents and it will certainly work for us! It is important to note that, research shows, most so-called "value education" exercises or courses in "moral reasoning" do not affect children's behavior, and in fact they tend to leave children morally confused and adrift. We don't have to add new theory courses to our school or church curriculumn or reinvent the wheel. We already have a wealth of information to draw from in material that most schools once taught to shape character. What was wrong with highlighting the character of individuals in history? Why not point out that Abraham Lincoln was 14 before he learned how to read, and look where his determination took him! That same self-control enabled him to study by candlelight and acheive a law degree through correspondence courses. His honesty compelled him to walk three miles to return six cents. How about the contrasting stories of "King Midas" and "The Little Engine That Could"- they contrast greed verses effort and determination. There are stories of ordinary folks who put aside their life to serve the military, coast guard, national guard or reserves in order to preserve our freedom. There are policemen and firemen who protect us around the clock, and farmers who work long days each week so that we always have food to eat. There are stories from the Bible that can be included as well: Ruth's loyalty to Naomi; Joseph's forgiveness of his brothers; the Good Samaritan's kindness to a stranger. We read in the Bible about the magnanimity of Elijah, leading horses and royal chariot of a defeated and dismayed Ahab to the gates of Jezreel in the storm God created to destroy Ahab. We learn in the Bible of David's cleverness in facing Goliath. There are a thousand examples at our beck and call, both in the secular and religious world, that emphasize positive personality traits.

The apostle Paul wrote, "Do not be misled: bad (evil) company corrupts good character (manners)." (See I Corinthians 15:33) What is character? The dictionary tells us that character is "moral or ethical strength; integrity." Yet, in defining good character, as the Bible suggests, we should include traits such as honesty, kindness, fidelity, diligence, fairness, courage, moderation, thoughtfulness, respect for others and much more. (See II Peter 1:5-7) True character is something that has to be cultivated as a child grows without being over-protected. They need the opportunity to develop strong character on their level. However, they are like trees; if everything goes their way, they will not develop the strong roots needed to survive against the heavy storms of life. On the other hand, teach them that life happens, and then provide the necessary guidance for them to meet the challenges of life, and to develop strong roots entwined with the rocks of knowledge to weather everything they encounter. By exposing our children to good character and inviting it's imitation, we will help them develop good character for themsleves.

In the business of character building, there is nothing more important than the quiet power of example. You would be surprised about the negative impact soap operas have on children aged one through five. Even when they appear not to listen, their ears are wide open and their mind is recording all that information into their memory. Unfortunately, their mind is not developed enough at that age to be able to discern what is real and not real, what is right and what is wrong. They accept all they see and hear as being real life, and not just stories.

We must never forget that true parenting is teaching our children, without fear, to think for themsleves. Help build confidence, self-reliance, insight, and the courage in which to face the world. No enemy of mankind has caused more misery and unhappiness than fear. It cripples constructive effort; it prompts cowardly actions and words; it produces confused and frantic minds; it results in sleepless nights; it expresses itself in selfishness, thoughtlessness and greed; it paralyzes the will; it destroys inner unity; it upsets physical health and shortens lives. A great American President, FDR, once said, "We have nothing to fear except fear itself." That was excellent advice in 1941, and certainly is appropriate with the current problems facing this country. However, we must not confuse fear with caution, which is that innate instinct that often helps us avoid real dangers. Moreover, we must teach our children that walking away from a confrontation is strength and not weakness. In the Bible, Romans 12:20 addresses the fact that treating an enemy with kindness is like putting hot coals on their head. Caution and fear are diametrically opposed to each other. Caution is necessary in successful living, while fear is a constant obstruction to it!

It is obvious that living without fear is a vital factor in Christian living. Christ put emphasis on overcoming fear (with confidence- building) during His short ministry. To His disciples, who were anxious concerning the material things of life, He said, "Oh ye of little faith." (See Matthew 6:30). When they were beset by a great tempest and mountainous waves, "Why are you fearful, O ye of little faith? (Matthew 8:26) Christ explained, when extending His hand to save Peter (who had walked toward the Lord on the sea until he became afraid), "Oh thou of little faith, why didst thou doubt?" (Matthew 14:31)

We cannot find better encouragement than His departing words... "Peace I leaave with you; my peace I give unto you; not as the world gives, give I unto you. Let not your hearts be troubled, neither let it be fearful." (John 14:27) In I Corinthians 10:13 we read that we will not be confronted by anything that is not uncommon to man, but that God is faithful and we won't face anything that we can't endure; also, we learn that God will provide a way out so that we can bear whatever we are suffering. The fear of failure can handicap anyone, especially the young who have not yet proved themselves. Failure conjures up terror of school examinations, undue shyness with others (especially those of the opposite sex) and countless variations of these bug-a-boos. Humans tend to dwell far too much on that nasty "F" word, "failure," letting it control their life. God did not intend anything in life to be negative except an electron. Failure is nothing more than a road sign, a brief setback, or a learning step in our life. Be positive, set those things in the past, and reach for what is ahead. (See Philippians 3:13) Moreover, a lack of confidence can tend to develop a follower personality. These individuals are usually passed over for promotion and can be prone to joining a gang or keeping up with fads, because they don't realize that they are "one of a kind," "they are important," and that they are a "needed and loved family member." The character of an individual is not measured in terms of victory or defeat, but the manner in which we approach each task. We must confirm to our children that life happens, that we can grow stronger from the experience, and that we all should glance in the mirror occasionally and take inventory of our self. (See James 1: 22,23 and II Corinthians 3:18) Each of our undertakings is to be accomplished in a quiet, prayerful humility, always striving to do our best. God expects no more than that from anyone.

We must entrust our children, and ourselves, to focus on the truth, things that are honest, pure, lovely, and of good report. (Philippians 4:8) That is important in every aspect of life, and especially during the pre-marital and marital period of our life. Marriage has been well-defined as "the first two-party system of government ever devised." This is a good definition because marriage was never intended to be a one-sided affair. (Ephesians 5:21) Of all human relationships, marriage is the most important. (Colossians 3:17-23) Only our relationship with God takes precedence. (Ephesians 6:6, 7) There is far too much at stake and no one should be tempted to enter into marriage lightly. Someone once said, "When God replied to Moses that He was, "I AM," the shortest sentence ever was created. Conversely, they said (with humor, of course!), that "I Do" is the longest sentence! While we can laugh at that observation, we must also understand its validity. We must remember that happiness, like courtesy, is a contagious quality. Happy couples create happy homes; happy homes produce happy children, which in turn contributes to happy communities, which can lead to a happy world- it all starts in the courtship stage of a relationship.

It always takes two people to make a successful marriage; unfortunately, it only takes one, through neglect or selfishness, to destroy it. True marital happiness depends not only on whether the individuals are well-matched, but also on whether they can live together with enduring affection and love. A happy and successful marriage means two entirely different individuals have blended their lives, allowing them to accomplish things together that would have been impossible for them to achieve alone. In other words, they have become compatible in thought (wants/need), word (communication) and deed (goals). God made us all different: unique as a snowflake and like beach sand- part and particle of everyone and everything we come in contact with. (Genesis 2:7) There is a book about men coming from Mars and women coming from Venus that discusses differences in men and women. Even if that analogy is representative, there are still similarities that permit growing and maturing together. We certainly prove that by growing up in a family environment from the stage of infancy to adulthood.

The Apostle Paul applies the second greatest commandment, by example, to four relationships that are essential to the happiness of a home: husband and wife, parent and child, employer and employees, and Christ and the Church. (See Ephesians 5:22- 6:7) By design, these Scriptures inder that the last example I listed should be the pivital point for the first three rules of living. (See Romans 12 and 13) We have already discussed the parent-child relationship. In marriage, we are to be joined together and spiritually become one flesh. As Christ was appointed the head of the Church, so has the husband been designated the head of the household.

Not as a tyrant or dictator, but rather in a leadership role, with responsibility and accountability. Try to imagine, God forbid, a baby being born with one body and two heads with individual brain and nerve systems. Just think of the compatibility, tolerance and understanding they would need to survive together. We certainly couldn't begin to fathom the difficulty, stress, duress and problems that would ensue if they went around doing their own thing. However, we can duplicate it in our marriage, and unfortunately many do. Consider, if you will, the work structure without a CEO, production plan, open communications, quality control, adequate line supervision, and workers who care. It is obvious that self-destruction and bankruptcy would occur in a very short time. By comparison, we are enjoined to be Christ-like in the other three relationships. He put others first; He was compassionate, understanding, re-spected His followers and higher authority. He went about doing good and healing all that were oppressed. (See Acts 10:38) He communicated with God often, and remained steadfast in His mission to the very end by saying, "Not my will, but Thy will be done." The Church, with the help of disciples, is Christs' most important "product."

In a family, the father is entrusted to be the mediator (coach and referee), with a deep understanding of the needs and opinions of the whole family. (See I Corinthians 12:12-27) Mindful that it is not healthy for one person to issue all the directions and make all of the plans, a variety of viewpoints, from all family members, are always helpful. However, this may produce a few tense moments. (Romans 12:3) That's alright: exasperation is a God-given emo-tional outlet, and a sort of "safety valve" to our tea kettle. Sin only occurs when anger develops without its being resolved and forgiven. (See Ephesians 4:26; Colossians 3:

110

13; and Mark 11:25, 26) On this basis, children will become good citizens by learning to respect authority in its many forms; the parents, the principal and teachers at school, the police, bosses in the work place, and throughout their lives, the government. Also, for a head start in their adult life, include your children in the budget process when they are old enough to grasp the importance and function of money. Encourage them to save by taking the time to explain the need to save or invest money for a rainy day. Bring them into the discussion of setting money aside for vacation, entertainment, or the need to buy new items and plan for it. You will find it easier for them to accept a "No" response for items on their "like to have" list. An important benefit will be the feeling of belonging and family unity they will get from that simple process.

Biblically, there is nothing wrong in being rich or accruing a lot of money. In fact, many of the people in the Bible stories were very prosperous. Contrary to what folks say, the Bible does not discourage planning ahead, either. The whole Bible is a master plan from God to bring redemption to mankind. From the beginning of time, to the destruction of Jerusalem, that plan is provided for all. If you need a specific example, just think on Noah and the Ark. Skeptics taunt the uninformed with false statements like, "How were the animals and seeds able to reproduce after all that time afloat?" and, "Surely Noah and his family had to eat something." That they did, because God provided for it when He told Noah to take food aboard to feed them and the animals. (See Genesis 6:21) In addition, God told Noah to take clean (eatable) animals and fowls of the air by sevens, and not just pairs as he did with the unclean. (See Genesis 7:2,3) We are not to worry (to get stressed out) about tomorrow, because the evil of today will keep us busy enough. (For reference, see Matthew 6:34) That doesn't imply that we should not plan for our tomorrows. Money, or having material items, is not evil; however, they are the driving force or the source for most ills and evil that has, will, and will continue to confront mankind. In Matthew 16:26 we read the question of what it profits a man if he gains the whole world but loses his soul? Instead of a controlled and balanced plan for saving and spending, people become slaves by letting money become their controlling force, just as the rich man spoke of in the Bible. (See Luke 18:18-23; Mark 10:17-22; Matthew 19:16-22) We snicker at the reaction of folks who had their idols destroyed in the Bible or in the movies that we watch. What would be your reaction if someone said you had to cut up your credit cards or have to drastically curtail your eating habits? Yes, folks, we have idols in this day and age that we need to place less importance on. No man can serve two masters. In Matthew 6:24 we see how we will either hate the one and love the other, or hold to one and despise the other; God and money cannot both be served.

God said, talking with those around Him, "Let us create man and woman in our image, after our likeness; in the image of God created He him, male and female He created them to multiply." (Genesis 1:26-28) He gave the male outdoor and woman indoor plumbing to facilitate that mission. That development, among other things, included testosterone in the male, and estrogen in the female, to provide control of secondary sex characteristics. How we thoughtlessly use, and misuse, God's gift, appears to come from behavior or social environment conditioning. Let it suffice to say that the mind (brain) is a powerful and informational force that controls all of our body functions. It goes without saying that a brain (being like a computer and

112

being very pliable), by the very nature of its purpose, can be subject to poor programming. God gave us that freedom of choice and the Bible to provide the programming and guidelines for our life. Therefore, we are part and parcel of everybody and everything we come into contact with. Our behavior can come from the most insignificant fears and events that occur in our youth. Therefore, it is the task of each individual to figure out who is putting thoughts into our head... God or Satan.

A complete study of sexual orientation is beyond the scope of this essay. However, it is appropriate to clear up a Biblical misconception of homosexuality that prevails in today's society. Maybe, this will provide you sufficient food for thought about your own beliefs and human prejudices without all of the extra study. The Bible tells us that eunuchs come from essentially three sources: from the womb, those that are man-made, and from choice. (See Matthew 19:12) God is not a respecter of persons in that He does not show favoritism or discrimination among the righteous. (See Acts 10:8,34; Romans 2:11; Galatians 2:6; and Ephesians 6:9) In John 1:12 we read that as many as receive Christ and believe in His name are given the power (right) to become the sons of God. At one point when God was talking to Isaiah in the Old Testament it was made clear that eunuchs were not excluded, saying, "neither let the eunuch say, "I am a dry tree;" keep my Sabbaths, choose the things that please me, and take hold of my covenant; even on them will I give a place in my house." (See Isaiah 56:3-5) In the New Testament, we find Phillip being dispatched to interept a eunuch returning to Ethiopia. After answering his questions and instructing him, Phillip immersed him in water and he became a member of

Christ's Church. (See Acts 8:27-39) God has no problem with those who choose not to marry and who provide joy to parents and relatives. God has no problem with like-sex individuals living together and sharing a life. He does not, however, condone or accept sexual relations between like sexes. (Romans 1:26-32)

For that matter, He doesn't approve of all the acts between hetrosexuals, either. When you are tempted to cup that hand and point that finger at someone, remember, there are three pointing back at you and the thumb points upward to God. It is not our place nor authority to judge that which we may suspect. God knows the truth and is the prevailing judgement authority to handle these problems. If we go about forbidding people from our place of worship, we are the bigger sinner. Let us not be guilty of assuming and passing judgement on individuals who are different than us. (See Luke 6:37)

People can become so obsessed with money that greed (keeping up with the Jones'), living beyond their means and all sorts of other evil can become a way of life that is hard to retract. (See I Timothy 6:6-10) That quicksand trap of life is called compound interest. Did you know, by making only a minimum payment on a credit card with a significant balance, it could take thirty to forty years to pay it off (depending on the interest rate, of course)? More importantly, those items you charged, even if they were on sale, may cost you ten to twelve times their original price before you reach a zero balance. On the flip side, did you know that it is possible to set aside a token twenty-five dollars a week in a retirement plan for yourself, for a short twenty-year period and accumulate $91,121, provide two children with $10,000 a year for college ($5,000 twice a year from that amount) over an eight-year period, and still acquire an additional $600 in your retirement fund?  Of course, if you continue on for an additional 30 years, that retirement fund would grow to $3,000,000!  Bear with me; I know the concept is hard to comprehend right now, but in due time you will understand it fully.

It is important that every family member appreciate and understand that we must first seek God's Kingdom and righteousness and all things will then be given to us. (See Matthew 6:33)  Equally important, they must all learn the upside (savings and investments) and the downside (loans, credit cards, etc.) of compound interest.  The doorway of the magic of compound interest is to understand what is called the "rule of 72!"  By dividing the number 72 by the % of interest will provide a point in time where your money will have doubled.  For example, 72 by 3%= 24 years;  72 by 6%= 12 years;  73 by 12%= 6 years;  72 by 18%= 4 years;  72 by 24%= 3 years.  It is as simple and uncomplicated as it appears.

If you took $2,000 and deposited it at 3%, after 24 years it would be worth $4,000;

If you took $2,000 and deposited it at 6%, after 24 years it would be worth $8,000;

If you took $2,000 and deposited it at 24%, after 24 years it would be worth $512,000.

You can see, at 6% the money doubled at 12 years to $4,000, and that doubled again by the time it reached 24 years.  At 24%, it doubled 8 times, to $4,000 at 3 years, $8,000 at 6 years, $16,000 at 9 years, $32,000 at 12 years, and each 3 year period for 24 years.  I am sure you can see that, while compound interest can make you rich

115

over time, it can also make or keep you poor if you over-use credit cards or loans. The same 18% that can generate $128,000 can cost you that much for a $2,000 purchase that is paid off at the minimum rate of $10.00 per month. So you have a card that only charges 12%; that $2,000 purchase will cost you $72,000 at the minimum payment of $10.00 per month. The next time you receive a credit card statement, look at the payment you made last month and see how much was applied towards the principle. You will see they always get their interest first. After all, a credit card company, bank, or any lending institution's only product is money. They stay in business by paying you a low interest on your savings account and charge three, four or even eight times that low rate for loans or extended payments.

I realize that credit must be used to purchase high-ticket items like a HOME. You can still minimize the interest bite by paying additional money, over and above the payment, on the principle. Even a small amount each month will save thousands of dollars over the life of the loan. A side benefit is that you will pay your mortgage off early. Above all else, do not purchase mortgage life insurance on a house or any other purchase. Ensure that your primary life insurance covers the breadwinners' loss of income. I can't overstress the need to establish a savings plan and take advantage of time. Just a dollar a day (thirty a month) when you are twenty-five at 12% interest will give you $296,516 by the time you reach sixty-five. If you wait until you are twenty-six, you will only save $264,402 or $32,114 less. At age thirty, $116,858; this shows how procrastination cost you $179,658! The longer you give it, the more compound interest works for you and/or against you. If nothing else, start an IRA with your tax refund in no-load mutual funds and have your work-place automatically deposit twenty-five dollars or more a week into the fund. With the tax advantage, you will hardly see a difference, and if you don't see it, you won't miss it!

In the secular world, we say, "the squeaky wheel gets the grease." The Bible says, "Ask and it will be given to you, seek and you will find, knock and the door will be opened." (See Matthew 7:7, 8) By using your God-given abilities, there are several areas where you can find extra money for a savings or investment account. If you consistently get a refund back from the IRS and State, fill out a W-4 form and increase your dependent status accordingly. You are not earning any interest while they hold your money, so it is the world's worst saving place. Instead of ordering a delivery pizza, pop one of the frozen store varieties in the oven and "doctor it up" with extra toppings that you like. If interest rates have dropped, review your home mortgage and compare rates. If you are paying three points (percent) or more above the current lending rate, it will be cost effective to lower your payment through refinancing. Give your current lien-holder first option to minimize the expense. Keep in mind, they are in the money business and don't want to lose your account. Talk to them first; if you contact someone else and are turned down, you have lost any bartering advantage. They will know, because your credit history will reflect the inquiry. If you are over your head in credit card debt, take the opportunity with a re-mortgage to pay them off by using some of the built-up equity. Don't do this unless you are disciplined enough to cut the cards up and then never use them again. A consolidation, in this manner, could be a tax advantage as well. Regular interest expense is not tax deductible, where a home mortgage can be. Check with your tax person for advice. If you don't consolidate credit

117

cards, call or write each current provider and given them an opportunity to lower your interest rate. Do likewise with the annual surcharge; get rid of that annual expense.

Life insurance is a paradox, and one of the worst gambles you can get involved in. The insurance company is betting that you will live forever and you are betting you will die young. However, the policies are necessary to provide income protection for the family in the event of an untimely death of the breadwinner. Or, you can view it as necessary until the time you can get enough saved that you don't need income protection. What is adequate protection depends on whom you ask and on individual circumstances. The normal rule of thumb varies from five to eight times your annual earnings. The best way to do that is avoid all of the policies with "bells and whistles." All you need is a simple 15 year Term Policy with a rider for the spouse and each child. You don't need extra policies for each; in fact, they cost you in operating fees as well as premiums. Take the difference between the term policy and the whole-life policy each month and deposit it in a mutual fund for the long haul. When shopping for term insurance, average the monthly payments out to ensure you are getting the best value. Some companies give a low first and second year rate and then sock-it-to-you for the next thirteen years. Also, make sure that the premiums will not increase during the term of the policy. When you buy cars, appliances, electronic devices, etc., avoid the extended warrenty package. If anything is going to break down, it will probably happen within the factory warranty period. Most states have a lemon law to handle that persistant problem. Besides, with competition as it is in today's business world, manufacturers do not want an unhappy customer on their hands. So, place the money you save into a CD or money market fund for the bigger and better mousetrap they will come out with next year!

I know these few "hints" are not complete, but I pray they serve the purpose of getting you started on managing your money instead of having your money manage you. More-over, start family traditions that will continue for many years to come. Whatever course in life you take, do take care and above all, "Take care of those in your life!"

The terms Old and New Testament are derived from
Jeremiah 31:31-34 and Hebrews 9. The Old Testament
(OT) books are narratives of a nation, which was chosen
and nurtured by God to prepare mankind for the coming of
a Savior of the world. The precepts of this important event
can be found in the books of Genesis, Deuteronomy,
Judges, Psalms, Isaiah, Jeremiah, and Micah. In addition,
the people of this select nation were given the prophets and
Law of Moses to act as schoolmasters until the arrival of
that Redeemer. (See Galatians 3:19 and 24) The OT
contains thirty-nine books written over a period of approxi-
mately one thousand years by writers who vaired from
uneducated herdsmen to highly skilled priests and kings.
To facilitate understanding and easy reference, the OT is
normally divided into four parts: law, history, poetry and
the prophets. Contained within these thirty-nine books is
every feasible topic imaginable to humankind. There is
humor, murder, mayhem, mystery, in-law relationships,
brothers plotting against brother, physiology, psychology,
husband and wife relationships and communication problems. You name it, and you will find it... even giants roam-
ing the earth are mentioned!

The first section comprises the first five books of the OT,
Genesis through Deuteronomy. These are referred to as
the Torah, the Pentateuch, the First Five Books of Moses,
or the Law. Torah is the Hebrew name and the Jews considered these five books paramount since they contain the
Ten Commandments and the foundation of their nations'
history. The use of the term Pentateuch came into being
when Alexander The Great had all of the Hebrew writings
translated into Greek; this means, "five scrolls."

The next twelve books, Joshua to Esther, comprise the history section. We read here about many things: from the capture of the land in Joshua, the inital history of the early nation in Judges and Ruth, the divided kingdom in I Kings through Chronicles, and the exile in Ezra through Esther. Hebrew poetry is different from English poetry in that its stresses a balance of ideas rather than sounds, rhythms, and images. In the third section, there is a classical poem (Job), a collection of hymns (Psalms), a compilation of traditional wisdom (Proverbs), an ornate meditation on life and all its vanities (Ecclesiastes) and a love poem (Song of Solomon).

The fourth section contains the writings of the prophets of Israel and is divided into two groups, the Major Prophets (Isaiah through Daniel) and the Minor Prophets (Hosea through Malachi). The placement in one group or the other implies neither value judgement nor importance but rather is an issue of length. The Major Prophets are long and the Minor Prophets are short. This part of the Old Testament contains major prophesies of the coming of Christ. The book of Daniel provides the interpretation of a vision King Nebuchadnezzer had. This dream outlined the five nations that would control the Hebrew nation in the coming years. During the last occupation, God would establish a kingdom to stand forever and could never be destroyed. (See Daniel 2:31-44) Moreover, God promised Israel that someday He would make a new covenant (testament) with the people. At that time, He would "write the law upon their hearts and minds," instead of stone, like the ten commandments. They would no longer need to teach about Him, because all would know Him. (See Jeremiah 31:31-34). In addition, the 400-year separation (or the silent period of God not speaking to man) that occurred between the testaments was prophesied in Amos 8:11.

Isn't it interesting to find that some studies of secular history and science have also confirmed events in the Old Testament?

The New Testament (NT), in a collection of twenty-seven books, is an account of the man, Jesus Christ, spoken of in the Old Testament. He is the most important person who ever lived, and has influenced more lives and civilizations than anyone else. By the means of His life, mortal death, burial and resurrection, Jesus became the mediator, testator, executor, and heir under His own testament. (See Hebrews 1:2; 9:15-18; 10:14-22) In John 14:6 Jesus said, "I am the way, the truth, and the life: no man cometh unto the Father but my Me." Anyone can become a joint heir by believing and following Him. Jesus told the disciples that His was the blood of a Bull. (See Luke 22:20; Exodus 24:8; Hebrews 9:19) The New Testament books are normally divided into four sections: the Gospels, Acts, the Epistles (or letters) and Revelation.

The first section, called the Gospels (Matthew, Mark, Luke and John) consist of four accounts of the life of Jesus. The word Gospel means, "Good news," and should be remembered, lest you get confused when you encounter the use of a phrase "my or our gospel" in your studies. The first three books are considered synoptic, because they look at Jesus' life from a comparable point of view. All four convey Jesus' birth, ministry, death on the cross, His resurrection, post-resurrection appearances, and ascension. They also clearly indicate Jesus was a human being with a divine nature, with the same characteristics of any other human. He was intelligent, logical, creative, imaginative, consistent, and had common sense. He got tired, hungry, thirsty, experienced pain, and suffered. There were times that He was angry, upset, distressed, sorrowful, lonely, calm, patient, or infuriated. The last of these human qualities was very evident in His conflict with the "prominent religious people" of His day. While going about preaching, teaching, healing the sick, casting out demons, restoring sight to the blind, and raising the dead as signs for the unbelievers, Jesus denounced shame, greed and licentious living.

His activities eventually aroused the antagonism of the chief priests, scribes (lawyers), and some rabbis. They disliked his caustic reference to the legalism of the Pharisees, his contempt for form and ceremony, and His scorn for pomp and luxury. He referred to them as being stiffnecked, hard-of-hearing, hypocrites, grandstanding when they contributed an offering (with rambling praying openly in the streets or synagogues to bring attention to themselves), fasting with a sad face as an actor would, and getting caught up in showmanship and unnecessary pageantry so that spiritual values were neglected. (See Matthew 6:2,5,7, and 16) Jesus rightfully accused them of not practicing what they preached, enlarging their phylacteries (a small box that hung around their neck containing the law of Moses) and the borders and hemlines on their garments to proclaim their pious self-importance. (See Matthew 23:3-6) He also chastised the leaders for leading the converted into damnation. (See Matthew 23:15) In Matthew 21:13 we read about Jesus confronting people using the temple as a business place and for activities not related to spiritual needs. He warned the general populous that unless their righteousness exceeded that of the scribes and Pharisees, they wouldn't enter the Kindgom of Heaven. Jesus used direct communication of the truth without hedging, calling a spade a spade. He was a master at using metaphors, analogies, parables, paradoxical statements, and other imagery to bring the truth to life. He even resorted to using figures of speech to wake up or shock listeners into self-examination. Good examples are, "If your hand offends you, cut it off;" or "if your eye offendes you pluck it out;" or telling the rich man he had to sell everything he had.

The message provided for us is that life should not consist of what we possess, our status, our pious acts, human efforts, being judgmental, or our self-fulfillment, but rather loving God and our neighbor, cultivating spiritual qualities of meekness, purity, compassion, righteousness and mercy. Only when we love God and our neighbor can we appreciate the intrinsic value of each individual, what God created, and ourselves.

Jesus went so far as to convey what method He would use to separate those who are His from those who are not by how they have treated others. Do we visit the sick, feed the hungry, clothe the naked, and give drink to the thirsty or welcome stangers? (See Matthew 25:31-46) More important, if we trust in what Jesus taught, we will achieve completeness second to no other. Our entire life, talents, interests, requirements, needs, dreams, plans, and values are included. Nothing is left out when we lose our life for the sake of Christ and the Gospel; we find the "pearl of great price" in a new and comprehensive way. (See Matthew 14:46) The Gospel makes it clear that Christ included the following among His basic teachings: the fatherhood of God and the brotherhood of man, the Golden Rule, forgiveness and love of one's enemies, repayment of evil with good, self-denial, condemnation of hypocrisy and greed, opposition to ceremonialism as the fundamental nature of

125

religion, the end of the First Covenant and the introduction of the New Covenant, the resurrection of the dead and the establishment of the Kingdom of Heaven, that man is a sinner by nature and can be saved only by faith and the grace of God through the redemption that is in Christ Jesus. Because Marks' is the shortest of the four Gospels, it is often recommended to a new student of the Bible as a starting point. It should also be pointed out that Luke was a physician, who traveled with the Apostle Paul. Luke's book was probably written from interviews taken when he traveled with Paul or was absent for brief periods. These absentee periods can be noted in the Book of Acts with the use of "they" in the third person in lieu or "we," as he wrote the book. Chapter 15 of Luke is often referred to as the "lost and found" section of the Bible.

The Book of Acts (which is like a "Part Two" to Luke) is also written by Luke. Essentially, it starts where the Gospel of Luke ends, with the apostles waiting in Jersusalem as Christ directed. (See Luke 24:47-53) It contains the history of the early church from Jesus' ascension, the arrival of the comforter (Holy Spirit), to the imprisonment of the apostle Paul in Rome. In Acts, we can follow the adventures and ministries of Peter and Paul, starting first in Jerusalem, then in Judea and Samaria, and to the other parts of the world. (See Acts 1:8) Acts contains several significant events that are only found therein. The first and foremost is a miracle that starts the spread of the Church and the Good News. Some Bible studies say that, when Peter gave his first sermon, interrupters were used to cover the language differences of the seventeen or eighteen areas of the Jewish world in attendance. Common sense tells me that it was a bigger miracle than we give it credit for. It isn't recorded how many were in attendance; however,

126

three thousand were converted on the first day and the Lord added to their number daily. (See Acts 2:41,47) I submit to you, as each apostle spoke, each person heard that speaker in his or her own language, and not the language coming from the speaker. In other words, the Holy Spririt translated the words at each pair of ears and not from the speakers' voice. Here is what the Bible says, "the multitude came together, and were confounded, because every man heard them speak in his own language. They were all amazed and marveled, saying one to another, "Behold, are not all these which speak Galileans? How hear we every man in our own dialect, wherein we were born?"" (See Acts 2:6-8, 11) Can you imagine the noise and confusion if seventeen or eighteen speeches, all in different languages, were being delivered all at the same time?

The organization of the Church that Christ built is very simple. The early congregations met in the homes of their members and listened to the spiritual testimony of various brethren who were in direct communication with the Holy Spirit. No distinction between laymen and clergy was recognized. Each independent congregation had elders whose function was to preside at the services, discipline members, and dispense charity. All the ceremonial gadgetry, dress, pomp and circumstance were nailed to the cross. There was no need for instrumental accessories either, because the NT directs the members to speak in psalms, hymns, and spiritual songs, to make a melody in their heart to the Lord. (See Ephesians 5:19) You will read of Saul (Paul before his conversion) raising havoc persectuing this Church, then his trip to Damascus, and his conversion. During a study of Acts, you will be able to track Paul's three trips and figure out where he was when he wrote each letter. You may even discover there is a hint of a fourth trip also. It is in Acts

(Acts 11:26) that the disciples were called Christians (followers of Christ) first in Antioch.  In Acts 20:35, Paul closes his conversation with the elders in Ephesus by reminding them to remember the words of the Lord Jesus, how He said, "It is more blessed to give than to receive." This is the only place this quote appears in the NT and reaffirms what John says in the close of his book, "But there are also many other things which Jesus did; were every one of them to be written, I suppose that the world itself could not contain the books that would be written." (See John 21:25)  In Acts we discover that the Sadducees believed that there was no resurrection, as well as believing that there were no angels or Spirits.  We also learn that the Pharisees believed in those things.  (A good way to remember the difference is to remember this saying, "the Pharisees believed in the resurrection and angels and that is "fair you see;" the Sadducees didn't, that is "sad, you see!")  Much of the information in Acts helps to give the reader a better understanding of what they read in the Gospels and in some of the letters.

The third section contains the twenty-one letters of apostolic writers to specific congregations, or to Christians generally, explaining the teachings of Christ, and relating these principles to the everyday problems of the people.  It is important to note that Peter closes out his first letter, "the Church that is at Babylon salutes you."  In my opinion this suggests that the Babylon referred to in the Book of Revelation is Jerusalem and not Rome.  If your Bible says Rome in lieu of Babylon, then an editor or publisher changed it to reflect their own belief.

The apostle Paul wrote the majority of these letters (Romans through Philemon).  The book of Hebrews is also

128

considered by scholars to have been written by Paul. Four of his books (Colossians, Philippians, Philemon, and Ephesians) were written while he was in prison the first time in Rome. A memory aide can be used to recall this fact by simply taking the first letter of each book and form this little ditty, "Cite Paul's Prison Epistle's." Titus and I and II Timothy are considered to be pastoral letters and contain specific qualifications for Church leadership. The only place the word immortal is used in the Bible is in reference to God in I Timothy 1:17. Man is not immortal and can be subject to a mortal death as well as a spiritual death, often referred to as the "second death." (See Revelation 2:11; 20:6; 21:8) Paul closes out II Timothy with a reference to leaving someone behind sick while on his journey. I trust you can learn a lesson from this observation in that Paul couldn't heal his trusted worker in spite of him having all the powers or gifts granted by the Holy Spirit. This lends credence to the fact that those gifts were to convince the unbelievers that God was with the apostles. (See I Corinthians 14:22) In the letter to Jude, one can read about the dispute with the Devil over the body of Moses. That disagreement should serve as a clue on how you should react to unchristian-like people that confront you in daily activities.

Considerable debate took place over circumcision, because Israelites thought it was "first things first," and that the Gentiles had to be like them. The Israelites appeared to have difficulty understanding that religious circumcision was no longer necessary and definitely not a requirement for Gentiles. False teachers, taking advantage of the time necessary to promulgate the Gospel between Christ's resurrection and the destruction of Jerusalem, were coming out of the woodwork. As anticipated, itchy ears were receptive to any and all information, true or untrue, that was given by anyone declaring any religious connection. The problems were compounded because, like today, very few took the time to check Scriptures to verify the information. It required a lot of effort combating false doctrine as well as putting down doomsday messangers, by all of the apostles, to keep the Christians upbeat, confident, and focused on the truth; much like today. Considerable effort was placed on several topics we need to revisit often: judging others; lawsuits; personal grievances; marriage problems; the human freedom to act as we please and the guidance to achieve our goals; baptism for the remission of sin at an age when we are cognizant of the difference between right and wrong, and not just for admission to a specific religious belief; and participating in the Lord's Supper on the first day of the week, every week. Paul had to remind the Corinthians that the Lord's Supper was not an occasion for a party in which to overeat and get drunk, but rather, the bread and fruit of the vine were to be small portions, the greatest element being spiritual, confirming that man does not, "live by bread alone." Paul also encountered a return to other pagan rituals in his travels and encouraged his followers to beware. He also warned of a dominant practice that was not ignored, and was in fact embraced later as is read about in I Timothy 4:1-7. A study of the Bible and secular history will confirm that a lot of what we encounter in various church services comes from pagan rituals and not from God's design.

A thumbnail sketch of the New Testament will confirm that Christ was designated in advance as the Savior of the world. (I Peter 1:20) One of His objectives was to reveal and give man a definite and tangible idea of what kind of "person" to reflect on when we think of God.

(See John 1:1,14,18) After the spread of His doctrine, there was no longer a need for religious circumcision or for the Law. (See II John verse 9; Romans 3:25-30 and 13:9; Ephesians 2:15; Colossians 2:14; and Galatians 3:24-25) Christs' purpose was to redeem people from their sins (Mark 10:45); relate sympathetically to their needs (Hebrews 2:17,18); to show that righteousness and justice are the foundation of Gods' throne (Psalms 97:2); to show that God doesn't discriminate (Colossians 3:25); to reveal that good fortune comes to the evil as well as the good (i.e., misfortune befalls the just and the unjust as we see in Matthew 5:45); to show that good gifts come from above (James 1:17); to show our suffering comes from Satan (II Corinthians 12:7); to show that pain is necessary, lest we continue to hurt ourselves; sickness is necessary to stimulate research; and most importantly, Christ was made perfect through suffering (see Hebrews 2:10); and to show that our difficulties will make us perfect, established, strengthened, and settled (I Peter 5:10). Moreover, by grace our weakness will strengthen Christ. (See II Corinthians 12:9) How? By our capactiy and ability to comfort others (II Corinthians 1:3,4); by putting others first (Philippians 2:3,4); by acquiring a better understanding of fellowship (Philippians 23: 1,2); by gaining a new appreciation for redemption (Romans 8:28,29). After all, if life was perfect, would Heaven have the same appeal?

Today Christ is alive, and sitting at the right hand of God, for the purpose of representing and interceeding for us. (See Romans 8:34; Hebrews 7:25; I John 2:1) He, and He alone, is our one and only mediator, our direct link to God in prayer or for the confession and forgivness of our sins. No other man, in Heaven or on earth, has been given that authority. (See I Timothy 2:5) By the successful completion of His work on earth, He is exalted to the Head of the church, and no other man, in Heaven or on earth, has been given that position either. (See Ephesians 1:22; 4:15) Through the NT and by the Spirit, He directs the life and service of all His saints (you and me) on earth. (See Matthew 28:20) We are remanded to walk in the Spirit and set aside those habits that corrupt the soul. (See Galatians 5:16-23).

Christ was not just a messanger of God, like the ancient prophets, but the eternal Son of God, presented and clothed with a human nature, and yet free from sin. He had a combinded human and divine nature.

The purpose of Jesus' baptism was the fulfilling of all righteousness, and identifying with those He came to redeem. (See Matthew 3:15) In this Christ exercised the first rule of leadership, "Do as I do," and lead by example. In considering the number of Passovers that occurred, His public ministry was certainly in excess of two years and probably no more than three. (See John 2:23; 5:1; 6:4; 13:1) But what a productive and beautiful legacy He left behind! He even gave us a format for our prayers in the Lord's Prayer in Matthew 6. In this prayer, Christ addresses several things that are important about prayer: it should be addressed to God; it is recognition that God is our sacred and supreme Being; it helps us remember that the kingdom is here; it is appropriate to pray for an increase; to give thanks to God for our blessings; to pray for our daily needs; to pray for forgiveness for evil we have done and the good we have left undone; to pray for us to forgive our debtors; to pray to be able to resist temptation and delivered from the evil one; to recoginize that God's Kingdom and power and glory are forever and ever. How should we pray? With faithfulness (James 1:6), with sincerity (Matthew 6:5-7), submissively (Matthew 26:39), unselfishly (James 4:3), with understanding (I Corinthians 14:15) and always in Jesus' name (John 14:13,14).

The fourth section is the Book of Revelation, a book about God's victory. This book is also referred to as the Apocalypse. The book is a fuller clarification of Chirst's dialogue of things to come. Revelation sets three time frames: things John had seen in the past, things that are in the present, and things that will soon be in the future. It depicts a vision experienced by the apostle John, in which he is given a message by God to be conveyed to the church. In this vision, he is given a view of Heaven, the throne of God, and Jesus as the triumphant leader of angelic forces against Satan and the forces of evil. While it appears to be cryptic in attitude, to the Old Testament people to whom it was written, it says a lot in a short writing, much as Christ's reference to the twenty-second Psalm did as Christ died on the cross. Revelation abounds in expressions used by Jesus during His brief ministry, while many of the metaphors are drawn from the Old Testament. Dating this book, and identifying what was to be destroyed, has created some of the greatest Biblical controversies of all times.

Looking at the pomp and ceremony of religious ceremonies on TV, hearing the never-ending ramblings on topics that are popular but untrue, and having read the disappointment, frustration, and anger Jesus had in dealing with the pious and self-important people of His time, I can't help but wonder what His reaction would be if He walked among us today? Would He be able to give our Christian leaders the courage to fess up, abort all the superfluous

133

pageantry, and return to the plain and simple teaching He established? Forgo pride and admit, one to the other, that there is truly one body (Church), one Spirit, one Lord, one faith (Christian), one baptism (immersion), and one God and Father. (See Ephesians 4:4-6) Are we so en-trenched that we fit into the category of the blind leading the blind? (See Matthew 15:14) How can anyone read Scripture and see that they are wrong and still return to teaching error? (See II Peter 2:21, 22) Didn't Adam and Eve commit the first sin by doing what God told them not to do? Shouldn't we let the Bible explain itself and do away with man-made theories? All of these issues, while important to the world, are beyond the scope of this essay. Yet, they document the importance of understanding the Bible and the will of God for all mankind. I would be remiss if I didn't provide a reminder that each person is alone responsible for their own salvation. However, there is a lot of help in the Bible and in Bible study groups to assist you in reaching that goal. In comparison to the time and effort it takes to retire from our earthly jobs, the time and effort to secure eternity is minuscule. Christ assures you that His "yoke is easy and the burden is light." (Matthew 11:30) As you walk in the Spirit, just apply a little common sense, think before you act or react, pray, plan ahead, and take one day at a time. Don't gener-ate any stress worrying about tomorrow, as there will be time to worry about it when it arrives; the stress of today will concern you enough. (See Matthew 6:34)

Many will tell you to read the Bible from front to back cover at least once a year. Some Bibles have even pro-vided a recommended study list. A friend or group may even suggest another. Whatever method you do choose, may I recommend the following "four W's" to you?

Please make note of four things: 1.) Who is writing? 2.) Why is the writer writing? 3.) What is the author writing about? 4.) Who is the writer addressing (the audience they are writing to)? Learn to pick up on little subtleties (clues, like in a detective book) as you read. For example, in the creation scene in Genesis 3:15, it reads, "And I will put enmity between thee and the woman, and between thy seed and her seed; it shall bruise thy head, and thou shalt bruise his heel." Seed is singular, meaning one, which is also confirmed by the use of "his." I am sure you already noted this was the first hint of Christ. While you are reading that verse, take a look at verses 21 and 22; verse 21 is significant in a study of baptism (whereas God clothed them as we are to be clothed by the water; i.e., immersed). Please note in verse 22, God is not alone indicated by the use of "us" when He says, "Behold, the man is become as one of us, to know good and evil; and now, lest he put forth his hand and take also of the tree of life, and eat, and live forever..." That tree of life, of course, is Christ. Note in the Book of Job, while Job thinks that his friends are God's messengers talking to him, they are in fact Satan's messengers. Luke wrote the book of Acts, but he was not always present. See if you can pick up on the times he was present or absent by the use of "we" or "they." When you respond to a Bible quote, read a couple of verses before and after the quote to ensure that it is not taken out of it's context (this applies also to my writings!)

We hear from the Bible every day of our lives. Some examples are: "late bloomer" (I Corinthians 15:8), "sour grapes" (Ezekiel 18:2), "split hairs" (Ezekiel 5:1), "doubting Thomas" (John 20:26), "the blind leading the blind" (Luke 6:39), "figs from thorns," "grapes from a bramble bush," and "blood from a turnip" (Luke 6:44), "the Lord gives and takes" (Job 1:21), "rob Peter to pay Paul" (II Corinthians 11:8), "skin of my teeth" (Job 19:20), "the spirit is willing, but the body is weak" (Matthew 26:41), "it's easier to put a camel through the eye of a needle, than for a rich man to enter Heaven" (Matthew 19:24), "live by the sword, die by the sword" (Matthew 26:52), "if you shed blood, then so shall your blood be shed" (Genesis 9:6), "Judge nothing before its time" (I Corinthians 4:5), "the love of money is the root of all evil" (I Timothy 6:10), "we brought nothing into this world, and it is certain we can carry nothing out" (I Timothy 6:7), "the right hand doesn't know what the left hand is doing" (Matthew 6:3), "entertain strangers, for you may have entertained angels unaware" (Hebrews 13:1), "garbage in, garbage out" (Matthew 15:11), "spare the rod and spoil the child" (Proverbs 13:24), "it is better to give than to receive" (Acts 20:35), "God loves a cheerful giver" (II Corinthians 9:7), "hand-writing on the wall" (Daniel 5:24), "thorn in the flesh" (II Corinthians 12:7), "be angry and sin not:  don't let the sun set on your wrath" (Ephesians 4:26), "blood money" (Matthew 27:6),  (Daniel 5:24), "thorn in the flesh" (II Corinthians 12:7), "be angry and sin not:  don't let the sun set on your wrath" (Ephesians 4:26), "blood money" (Matthew 27:6), "one day is like a thousand years to the Lord, and a thousand years as one day" (II Peter 3:8), "my lot in life" (like the casting of lots mentioned throughout the Bible), "babbling idiot" (referring to the confusion, when everyone's language was changed, at the destruction of the tower of Babel).  We also sing songs with Bible themes, as well. Some examples of these are, "Oh them dry bones, now hear the Word of the Lord" (Ezekiel 37:4), "Coat of many colors" by country singer Dolly Parton (Genesis 37:3).

You will be surprised how many expressions and songs are taken from the Bible when you read and investigate it in earnest. Remember, "there is nothing new under the sun." (Ecclesiastes 1:9)

I trust you will not let me lead you astray with all the emphasis on the New Testament and very little on the Old Testament in this essay. The Old Testament is history that should be studied in earnest as well. We need to study history to learn from other people's mistakes; if we don't, we will be inclined to repeat those mistakes. In the mean time, "May the peace of God, which surpasses all understanding, keep your hearts and mind through Christ Jesus." (Philippians 4:7)

## LIST OF POEMS

*Scriptures quoted in this book are from the King James Version of the Bible, if not otherwise specified.